S0-BCO-165

THE AQUEDUCT PAPERS

ABOUT THE AUTHOR

Brian Kingslake was born in 1907, in London England. Teen-age studies on the writings of Swedenborg led him to decide to enter the ministry of the Church of the New Jerusalem (Swedenborgian). He wanted first to see something of the world, believing (quite erroneously) that once he was an ordained minister he would have to settle down for life! So he travelled about, often vagabond fashion, in many parts of the world, ranging from Lapland in the north, to Zululand in the south.

In 1934 he graduated from the New-Church Theological College in Essex, England, and for the next sixteen years he occupied pastorates in the north of England. In 1950 he was sent out to South Africa, as General Superintendent of the large and expanding New-Church Mission. He occupied this position for twelve years, and was also Principal of the Mooki Memorial College in Soweto for training African ministers. And it was to help explain Swedenborg's vision of the Spiritual World to his students there that he first had the idea of an imaginary interview with "someone over there".

In 1962 Mr. Kingslake was transferred from Africa to America, and occupied pastorates in Philadelphia, Cleveland and Washington D.C. (He was in Washington during the upheavals of Watergate and the Vietnamese war.) In 1973 he retired to his native Britain, and has since been living in Bath, Avon. From his retirement he has published five books in addition to the Aqueduct Interviews: "For Heaven's Sake", "Out of this World", "Swedenborg Explores the Spiritual Dimension", "Angel Stories" and "A Swedenborg Scrapbook".

Mr. Kingslake's wife Jill is an Oxford graduate; they have three married daughters and ten grandchildren.

THE AQUEDUCT PAPERS

Twenty Interviews with an Angel
Concerning Life after Death

by Brian Kingslake

SEMINAR BOOKS
LONDON

THE AQUEDUCT PAPERS

Seminar Books
Swedenborg House,
20-21 Bloomsbury Way,
London WC1A 2TH.

First published by Christopher Publishing House
Boston, U.S.A., 1970
Reprinted by Seminar Books 1987

Copyright © Brian Kingslake
ISBN 0 907295 17 7

Seminar Books are published by
The Missionary Society of the New Church
and distributed by
New Church House, 34 John Dalton Street,
Manchester M2 6LE

Printed by Battle Instant Print Ltd.,
143 St. Georges Road,
Hastings, East Sussex TN34 3NF

Cover drawing by Charles Townsend

PRELUDE

"Vapor Trail"

There are men and women up in that jet;
A smartly-dressed air hostess moves among them
    Serving coffee.

To us, it is only a piece of white chalk
Curving a double line across the sky:
A moving finger, leaving a question-mark
    And vanishing.

Very soon their journey will be ended.
"Fasten your seat belts, and no smoking please!"
Then they will say good-bye to the smiling hostess,
And step out through the open doorway
    Into a new world.

In our sky, the question-mark slowly disintegrates
Into little wisps of cloud,
    And is forgotten.

B.K.

"Nothing is more delightful and blessed to the angels than to instruct those who came from earth into the other life."

Swedenborg

CONTENTS

Emanuel Swedenborg

EXPLANATION

The general conception of *Life After Death* presented in these pages has been drawn from the writings of Emanuel Swedenborg (1688-1772).*

Swedenborg was one of the most remarkable men of his age, or any age. After a distinguished career as Assessor of Mines in the Swedish government, and the production of a series of massive scientific and philosophical works on such far-reaching subjects as the structure of matter, the origin of the cosmos, and the physiology of the human body with special reference to the brain, Swedenborg experienced psychic changes which resulted in the quickening of his inner senses so that he could enjoy open vision into the world of the spirit. He "walked about" in heaven and hell, met old friends who had passed over, and visited familiarly with spirits good and bad, learning from them the conditions of their lives in minute detail. These experiences took place over a period of twenty-seven years, and during the whole of that time he lived a normal life on earth, writing voluminously, travelling extensively between the cities of Europe, correcting proofs, and taking his seat in the Swedish House of Nobles.

Swedenborg's books, written in Latin, are somewhat ponderous and repetitive, and many people find them difficult to read. My Aqueduct Interviews are intended to present his basic teachings on the spiritual world in an attractive, even whimsical, style, more accessible to the general reader who is hungry for information about the Great Beyond.

The Angel Aqueduct, himself, is a product of my imagination, and I have taken liberties in working up some of the details of these interviews. But what I have written

* Swedenborg's writings, including 'Heaven and Hell' in paperback, can be obtained from the Swedenborg Foundation, Inc., 139 East 23rd Street, New York, N.Y. 10010; or the Swedenborg Society, 20 Bloomsbury Way, London, WC1A 2TH, England.

THE AQUEDUCT PAPERS

is not mere fiction. This book contains, I believe, a real and true account of the kind of thing everyone will experience sooner or later when he or she passes through the gateway of death. I hope these disclosures will be reassuring, and that the contemplation of them will prove spiritually invigorating to the reader, as they have been to me in writing them.

Brian Kingslake

ONE

AQUEDUCT INTRODUCES HIMSELF

* This phrase is a kind of 'Signature Tune', indicating that the interviewer is on the correct wave-length for the interview.

Interview 1

AQUEDUCT INTRODUCES HIMSELF

Greetings, dear friend from the other side! How you
have come here, I do not know; and whether you will
be able to return whence you came, I do not know. All
of us in this world entered through one or other of the
Reception Buildings; and none of us, in my experience,
has ever returned! However, I know there can be ex-
ceptions to every rule, if the Lord in His mercy wills
it; and I am indeed grateful to Him for the privilege
of being able to communicate in this manner with someone in my old homeland.

The difficulty will be for me to convey my thoughts
to you in such a way that you will be able to interpret
them into your earth language, which (pardon me!)
seems so clumsy, since its sounds bear no relation to
the ideas expressed. Our language consists of the
thoughts and ideas themselves, clothed with sound. The
task will be hard for you, I fear; but you will just have
to do your best to receive my thoughts into your own
thinking mechanism, and then re-express them in your
own way in your own language, writing as of yourself.
We shall see how we get on.

To begin with, you want to know my name. Now, it
is a strange fact that although I have often tried to
remember the sounds which constituted the name I
bore on earth, they always elude me. This is because

17

they had no intrinsic meaning; they were merely vibrations in the air. Here I am called *Aqueduct,* in reference to my employment or function. The Lord has made me a channel through which a trickle of His Divine Truth can penetrate to the bewildered and thirsty souls who have just come over from your world by the process called death. In other words, *I am a Receptionist.*

You ask me to speak further about myself. Perhaps you do not realize how embarrassing it is for us to do this. There was a time, I have no doubt, when I should have been only too delighted to talk about myself, but now it gives me a cold feeling in the pit of my stomach. To relieve the depression, one must turn one's thoughts to other people, or better still towards the Lord; then one is happy again. However, for the sake of making our interviews more useful for your purpose, I will do my best to answer any questions you wish to ask.

Am I an angel? Well, if by angels you mean a special kind of superior being, with wings and feathers and harps, then I certainly am not an angel! Such creatures do not exist; or, if they do, I have not seen one. Here we are simply *people* — ordinary men and women, who once lived on your earth or some other earth like it. As far as origin is concerned, you and I are brothers; we were made from the same clay.

Do I live in heaven? Why yes, I live in heaven. The presence of the Lord makes heaven, and He is ever present with us. But my village is not altogether different from villages in your world. It is surrounded by a broad countryside of gardens and meadows and orchards and cornfields, with a view of woods and mountains beyond. I love it, and feel more at home in my neat little two-roomed house than I have ever felt anywhere else in my life. It is certainly heaven to me!

How long have I been over here? That is difficult to say, because we do not measure time as you do. Sometimes it passes quickly, sometimes slowly, depending on how busy or happy we are. There are no fixed days or years.

I do not think I could have been here long, by your reckoning, because my beloved wife has not yet joined me. That wonderful experience is still to come. I contact her frequently — especially when she is asleep; and from her thoughts I draw news from your world. This prevents me from altogether forgetting my former state, and may qualify me to some extent to work with those who have only just left your world and are still under its limitations. And the fact that I am still, as it were, anchored there, undoubtedly makes it easier for me to communicate with you.

I wish my wife could see me as I see her, but she is completely blinded by her involvement in her physical environment. With the deep love that is in her heart, she is still mourning my "death," and regards it as a dreadful disaster, whereas in fact it was a perfectly normal and orderly step in my development, according to our Heavenly Father's plan. She worries because she thinks I suffered during my final illness. Perhaps I did, perhaps I did not; I cannot remember. Most people wake up on this side as from a deep sleep, unconscious of any agony in association with their transition. Generally they think they are still where they were. My duty is to receive them, and explain to them, insofar as they will listen, that they have now entered their eternal life, and that they have left their physical bodies behind because they are of no further use to them. Many refuse to believe this, since they find they still have a head, body and limbs, and can see, hear, smell, taste and feel, even more keenly than before. They laugh at me and say I am crazy. There are some spirits who have been here for countless centuries of your time, yet they still hotly deny what they call "the continuation of life after death." They say that when they die they will be snuffed out like a candle! How can anyone convince them?

You ask me if I have ever seen God. In one sense, God is within us, but invisible. In another sense, He is up there in the sky. Look, you can see Him for yourself. That glorious and effulgent Sun is the Lord's first appearance in the finite universe. No finite being can see Him as He is in His Essence; but, in order to create the universe, He veils Himself in various atmospheres, and successively withdraws His power from Himself, until His Divine Substance becomes finite; and then we can see Him as the Spiritual Sun. From that Sun, all the heavens derive their substance, and the angels derive their life. From that Sun also come all the suns and stars in your physical universe, so the Spiritual Sun is the Source of your world also.

Our Sun varies somewhat in appearance in different regions. Those angels who love the Lord most ardently, see it as a vast flaming mass of red fire, directly before their faces. But that would be rather dazzling for us common folk, so we see it paler and whiter, and slightly to one side. For it is a fact (which most new arrivals find surprising) that whichever way we turn, the Sun always appears in exactly the same position in front of us — a position which has been established by our permanent inner relationship towards the Lord.

In this region where I work, alongside your world, there is some confusion in respect to the Sun, because the new arrivals have every kind of attitude towards the Lord, and so some see the Sun in front of them, and some behind, and some have it swinging from this side to that, as they try to make up their minds what their attitude really is! Part of my job is to help sort them out, and this is called the Judgment. I am told that the inhabitants of hell have the Sun perpetually behind their backs, and that they walk in their own shadows.

Does the Lord ever speak to me, you ask? Yes, indeed He does. Actually He is communicating with us all the time, sometimes by a clear inner voice, but usually by the pressure of thought and will. And once — something happened which was so wonderful I hardly dare speak of it.

I was walking along by the bank of a river with one of my brothers, engaged in deep conversation, when a Stranger joined us. In burning words He opened for us a whole new world of thought and vision. And when, almost swooning with excess of joy, we perceived who He was, He vanished away, leaving behind Him a lambent glow, an ineffable perfume, and the sound of celestial music. As we gazed rapturously around us, we saw that the countryside was covered, as far as the eye could see, with glistening flowers of all the colors of the rainbow — and so was my heart.

TWO

BALANCE-LAND

Interview 2

BALANCE-LAND

*This is Aqueduct speaking. Greetings, dear friend from
the other side!* I must apologize for the abrupt termination of our previous interview. This was entirely
due to my discourtesy. I was so caught up in the contemplation of our beloved Lord, that for a while I was
oblivious of everything else; and when I came to myself again, you had disappeared! I am truly glad you
have been permitted to return.

If I may say so without offence, you seem less spec-
tral and ghostly today than you were before. Do you
think you could sit on a chair, if I thought one up for
you? There! We will recline at ease under this wide-
spreading tree outside the reception hall. As you
see, new arrivals are continually passing out through
the gates. Some are literally dancing with the new-
found joy of life; others are bewildered and confused.
Soon I will go and offer my help; but, for the time being we are invisible to them, and they will not disturb
us.

You must understand that this is not my home, but
only the place where I work. It is neither heaven nor
hell, but the *middle region* in between. Over there to
the east and south stretch the heavens, covering the
hills and distant mountains, right to the skyline and
beyond. Ah, forgive me! My apologies; the sun is rath-

er dazzling in that direction! Many people cannot look there, except, as it were, out of the corner of their eyes. Rest your vision for awhile by looking to the west and north, where the ground drops away to a lower level! There lie the hells, under a perpetual smog.

Some of us call this place "Balance-Land," because it is like a pair of scales exactly balanced. Everyone who comes over from your world is at first in a state of equilibrium; but, as the *ruling love* which they developed while on earth begins to assert itself, they tip up the scales toward heaven or hell, and set off voluntarily in that direction. The Word of God, which we have over here just as you have, speaks of those who have been "weighed in the balance and found wanting"; and your ancients thought of the souls of the departed as being weighed in scales.

This Balance-Land lies alongside your world, which is why you have appeared to me here and not in heaven itself. All people in your world are living here as to their spirits, though normally they are conscious only in and through their physical sense organs. (You are the exception which proves the rule!) At death, when the physical body falls away, the soul remains where it always has been — which is, *here;* but the consciousness shifts over into it, and only then does it become fully visible to us.

You on earth owe your precious gift of free will to the fact that you are in this Balance-Land; and your spiritual equilibrium is always carefully maintained for you by the Lord. Only once, we learn, was this free will seriously in danger: the scales were tipping down toward hell and would not swing back. Then it was that the Lord Himself came to our rescue. He descended to earth as a Man among men, and restored the balance from your side. That was the Redemption — His greatest act of mercy; glory be to His holy name!

Your world and this Balance-Land are essentially the same world, and so they appear similar, whether seen from your side or ours. Here we have rocks and trees and rivers, flowers and birds and animals of all species, good and bad — the good from heaven and the bad from hell. Since this place is in equilibrium, things are bound to be mixed up here, as they are with you. Roses have thorns, and so on. Our world is the world of causes, yours is the world of effects.

We even have cities here, corresponding to yours on earth: the *concept* of the particular city is here — its essence, its flavor, its soul; whereas the bricks and glass and concrete are over with you. A man who dies in such-and-such a town, and has his heart there, naturally wakes up in it here. Which comes first: the city in this world, or the corresponding city on earth? The two are one! They grow and develop together.

Let me illustrate this by reference to the many scientific inventions which are apparently revolutionizing conditions on earth. Every one of them must come into existence here first, as a projection of the inventor's mind, before he is able to clothe it in material forms on earth. The prototype is here. Oh, you would be astonished at the weird contraptions which appear from time to time in this Balance-Land: vehicles for travelling across land or water or through the air, and now out into space; television and computers and every kind of device and gadget, most of them quite unintelligible to us! We do not need them ourselves. Always we have been able to fly through the air, without wings or other aids. We can communicate with people at a distance, and see them while we are speaking with them; and the Lord allows us to produce anything needful by an act of will.

We have been told that it is characteristic of the New Age which is dawning on earth, that your inventors are trying to reproduce, by scientific means, the conditions which we have always enjoyed here in the spiritual world. What we can achieve directly by an act of will, you are achieving in your environment by a clever manipulation of the subtle forces of electricity which underlie physical matter. We wish you well in this, provided only that you use these new techniques to help bring in, and not destroy, the Kingdom of God.

The main difference between your world and ours arises from the fact that physical matter resists change. You cannot move it or alter its form, without bringing physical forces to bear upon it. Here, our surroundings are pliable, and are shaped by our desires and needs, being instantly responsive to the minutest changes in our states. Our environment, in fact, is a projection of our thoughts and affections.

Why are the two worlds so different in this respect? Because they exist for different purposes. Your world provides for character formation; ours is for life itself. Yours is a training ground. Most of you start your adult lives on earth dominated by selfishness, impurity, and love of possessions (am I right?). If you had your own way in everything, as we have here, you would inevitably slide down into hell. But the batterings of an inflexible environment soften and change you; and, if you react to them wisely, the Lord is able to transform you from dross to pure gold. But, when you come over here through the gateway of death, that part of your preparation is ended. You have left school, and the discipline of school is relaxed. Here you can (and even must) do what you like. No longer are you the product of your environment. On the contrary, *you* are now the fixed and determining factor, and your environment responds to you.

When people first arrive in this world they are usually in a very confused condition, and must undergo a period of rest and convalescence before their personalities can operate freely. Often they are obsessed with fantasies and hallucinations arising from the circumstances of their deaths. One will think he is in an automobile accident, surrounded by the wreckage of his car, and will keep muttering: "That was a narrow escape!" Another will imagine he is drowning, and will keep shouting for help, until he feels loving arms bearing him up. The thoughts in which people die continue with them for a while, and are projected into their new environment, so there is no break in continuity, no shock of change. Most, when they first awake in this world, believe they are still in the old. My job is to explain to them what has happened. Once the true situation has sunk into their minds, the fantasy ceases, the hallucination disappears. The sick man leaves his bedroom; the car wreckage vanishes; the drowned man finds himself on shore in dry clothing. The incident of their transition is forgotten, and they settle down to the process of self-discovery, which will eventually take them to their final homes in heaven or hell.

None of these people remain very long with us in Balance-Land. Soon their inner nature begins to emerge. They are confronted with the Lord's divine mercy and love, and they instinctively react, either striving to receive it, or fleeing anxiously from it. The Lord's mercy comprehends everybody. Every created soul is intended for heaven, and there is a powerful drag towards heaven. Some resist this, but to me such resistance is incomprehensible.

When I first felt that divine tug and pull, I yielded to it as a lover yields to the embraces of a loved one. Not that I was particularly good. I had been a very ordinary person on earth. Actually, I was all too well aware of my weaknesses and imperfections, and fully expected to be cast into hell. Imagine my surprise when no particular notice was taken of my record, good or bad. I was not asked any questions, but was simply assured that the Lord loved me with divine compassion, forgave me all my sins, and willed only that I should go to Him, and be blessed and made happy by Him. Then it was that I joyfully relinquished all my own self-centered desires, and let Him take me where He would.

That urge to be with Him is coming upon me again, and is a sign that this interview must end. Please come back soon.

Good-bye, and God bless you.

THREE

SELF-JUDGMENT

Interview 3

SELF-JUDGMENT

This is Aqueduct speaking. Greetings, dear friend from the other side! It is indeed a strange experience for me to be conversing like this with someone who is still in the physical body. Usually, when we see such beings at all, they are merely wraiths or ghosts that vanish into thin air if we address them. But you, my friend, are almost as solid and substantial as one of us! Moreover, I find I can convey my thoughts to you with the utmost ease; and I learn from various sources that you have been able to express them very adequately in the language of earth — that peculiar sound-language so incomprehensible to us. Now that we have developed the techniques of our little experiment, I hope you will visit me quite often.

In our last interview, you asked me about this *waking-up* place which we call Balance-Land, and I began to tell you something of our work here. There are many centers like ours, and a large number of Receptionists, whose duty it is to receive the new arrivals from your world who have come through the doorway of death, and explain to them the conditions of their new life, and put them on the next stage of their journey. The work is highly interesting and rewarding, and I am forever grateful to the Lord for the privilege of being able to participate in it.

Nevertheless, one can become very depressed by the appalling number of people who insist on taking the road to hell, although we urge them and plead with them, and use every means in our power to try to persuade them to come up with us to heaven. That is the greatest of all tragedies — the only real tragedy: those warped, twisted souls, who are so obsessed with their own self-importance that they struggle frantically to avoid any possibility of involvement in love to the Lord or love to their fellowmen.

Fortunately, most of the new arrivals are good at heart and ready to learn; they are merely muddle-headed and confused. When they first realize where they are, they are usually overcome by a dreadful uneasiness of heart, which may amount to fear, even terror. They expect to be taken to a kind of police court and hauled before a harsh judge who will sentence them to everlasting punishment. Poor creatures! We do all we can to reassure them, explaining that God is their heavenly Father who loves them with an infinite tenderness — why should He want to harm His own children?

Many from the Christian world expect to be asked what church denomination they belonged to, and whether they supported it faithfully. Non-attenders pour out their excuses. Some are eager that we should catechise them on their doctrinal beliefs, thinking they will be saved by their faith. Others try to impress us with the many good works they have performed, the welfare committees they have served on, and the money they have given to charity. We let them talk! Some feel a compulsion to confess all the sins they have committed, and fall on their knees begging for forgiveness. Sometimes I suspect they are exaggerating, though

they may be thinking of the evils they would like to
have done, and would have done if they had had the
courage. When we tell them we are not interested in
how wicked they have been, they are indignant and
angry.

We explain that it makes no difference, now, which
church they attended, or did not attend, or whether
they were baptized, or took Mass or Holy Communion,
or whether they subscribed to any particular creed or
article of faith, or even whether they were Christians
at all, or Moslems or Buddhists or so-called heathens.
These things were important in the old life, but their
significance passes when you come over here.

Perhaps someone committed adultery in his youth,
or served a term of imprisonment for forgery, or drank
alcohol, or blasphemed against the Holy Spirit. All that
is finished, forgiven; it has been left behind with the
physical body in the grave. What people bring with
them into this world is nothing but *themselves*: their
underlying character, *as formed by* their religious and
social background, their actions good and bad, their
habits and beliefs, the complex of all their desires and
ambitions, all they have thought and willed and done
during their lives on earth. What they bring with them
is the quintessence of it, distilled and poured off.

We can read their characters like an open book. We
have only to look into their faces to discern their
ruling love. In fact, we can *feel* it by their reaction to
the love we have for them. But, even if we were entirely
ignorant of a person's character, we could soon guess
it by the way he behaved in the freedom of his new
life.

You will have noticed how difficult it is to deceive
or dissemble in the frank atmosphere of our environ-

ment here. Shams and hypocrisies fall away, as do all reserves and inhibitions. You no longer care what others may think of you; you just *have* to express yourself freely and openly. And so your actions judge you. No other judgment is necessary.

Strangely enough, as the new arrivals begin to act freely from themselves, their characters often appear to go into reverse. For example, some who lived highly respectable lives on earth, plunge into sin when they arrive here. This is because they actually cherished evils while in your world, and gave mental assent to them, only refraining from the open act through fear of the consequences, especially loss of reputation. Now they feel free to go ahead! On the other hand, some, who lived notoriously evil lives on earth, now become reformed characters. Perhaps they had got themselves into trouble through folly in their youth, or weakness of the flesh, or oversensitiveness to a bad environment and the influence of bad companions; but in their hearts they detested their evils, and despised themselves for yielding to them. When they wake up here, and find they are free to do exactly what they like, they are only too pleased to make a fresh start, unimpeded by the dead weight of their former bad habits and physical cravings. These examples, of course, are extreme cases. Most people come somewhere in between. But the principle is always the same: people judge themselves, by being exactly what they want to be, and doing exactly what they want to do. And the outcome is: heaven ... or hell.

Ask your friends over there: how would they be living now, if they could do what they liked, and had everything they craved for? A sincere and true answer to that question will indicate where they will be in their future life. Please warn them also that it is not only the conventional vices that will carry a man to hell. There are attitudes of mind encouraged by your society and held to be quite respectable, which may completely bar the way to heaven. I mean such things as aggressiveness, self-satisfaction, a sense of superiority and importance, jealousy and vindictiveness, over-criticalness, touchiness, a tendency to be easily offended, and that superficial busyness which wears itself out going round and round but never gets you anywhere. Sin can be defined as "that which separates a man from his heavenly Father." The various grades and species of self-love and love of the world may do this far more effectively than drunkenness, gambling or sexual indulgence. You people over there should reassess the seriousness of the different classes of evil. Otherwise it may be that, in trying to keep out of the frying pan, you will plunge right into the fire!

Excuse me one moment. Ah, do you see that small group of agonized men and women running away from us down the hill towards the west? They keep turning and shaking their fists. Listen, I can hear what they are saying as they go: they are pleading with the mountains and rocks to fall on them and hide them from the wrath of the *Lamb*. See, the earth is splitting and opening in front of them. The first few have reached the fissure and are leaping in; the others follow. Now they are all gone. The great crack in the earth which has received them is closing over them again.

My colleagues and I have been working with these poor folk for some time, trying to straighten out their minds, but it has been to no avail. *"The wrath of the Lamb!"* That has been their fantasy. They think they are being threatened by a baby sheep who is angry with them. It would be comic if it were not so tragic. The real position is that they cannot bear the sphere of perfect *Innocence* which surrounds our beloved Lord, and which is represented to them as a *lamb;* and they are so distorted in their own minds that they mistake the divine benevolence for wrath.

They will not be hurt by their fall. At the bottom of that crack in the ground are dark caverns in which they will rest for awhile. Later they will make their way along tunnels and underground passages which will lead them out into that low-lying region beyond the escarpment. There they will find communities of souls like themselves, with whom they will live in the way they want to live. The Lord is caring for them, as He cares for us all.

Now see that group on the other side of the reception buildings, those who are lifting up their eyes to the hills. It has been a real joy to work with them. I have promised to take them on the first stage of their journey, to a college over there to the east, and they are eagerly awaiting me, so I must leave you now and go and help them.

Good-bye, and God bless you.

FOUR

The Talking Woman

Interview 4

THE TALKING WOMAN

This is Aqueduct speaking. Greetings, dear friend from the other side! I am glad to see you, though I must confess that just at the moment I am feeling tired and frustrated. I have been struggling all day to help restore one woman to a proper relationship with her Maker, and have dismally failed. As this kind of thing happens quite often, and this woman is typical of many who come over from your world, I will give you a detailed account of the case, in the hope that it may serve as a warning to some, and help you and your people over there to see life more clearly in its proper perspective.

She was a cultured and intelligent woman, and when I first saw her this morning I thought I should get on well with her. She realized more quickly than most do that she had passed over into the spiritual world. Knowing that my job was to help her, she confided in me readily — far too readily, as I was soon to discover.

How that woman talked! It was a disease. Self-expression, the pouring out of her thoughts before they were properly formed, the bubbling over of her *ego* ... neither she nor anyone else could stanch the flow.

At first she was very charming. She showed an interest in my work, and said she would like to take up similar employment when once she had settled down. There

41

was nothing that would suit her better, she said; and she was well qualified for it, having devoted the whole of her life to helping other people. One thing only was worrying her at present — her three children. Two boys and a girl. Yes, of course, they were in their late teens, and an aunt would be looking after them; but they were all three so devoted to her, and they had always been so dependent on her — she just could not imagine how they would manage without her. She had always done everything for them, and protected them against their good-for-nothing father, who used to beat them when he had been drinking too much. When children have a father like that, the mother means more to them than usual — didn't I agree?

And so she went on to tell me what she had suffered from that man. He had been her "cross," which she had always borne with Christian patience and fortitude. She gave me a detailed account of incident after incident in which he had figured badly. She said she had written down all the facts in a notebook — she would show me one day. Once he had beaten her so hard that he had made a weal right across her back. She loosened her dress to show me the scar, but then suddenly realized she was now in her spiritual body and so would have no scar! But by making an effort of will she produced the effect of it, apparently to her great satisfaction.

It was not only her husband's drinking and cruelty, she said. What upset her most were the "other women." Oh, there had been a succession of them, who had insulted her to her face. Yet, for the sake of the children, she had always been patient and forgiving, and had never divorced him, though the cynical brute had often begged her to do so. "Forgive and forget"

was her motto. Of course (she said) I might not agree
with her. She might be wrong in holding to this, but
she believed it was a Christian's duty to forgive and
forget, which she had always done, even with that
husband of hers. What did I think?

She herself had devoted most of her time to child
welfare, as she was passionately fond of children. She
had been an inspector for an Orphanage Society which
put children out into private families. She was not
one of those people who were content to sit on committees; she actually went into the homes where the
children were boarding — slum homes, most of them.
Of course, she took some insect powder with her, which
she sprinkled on the chair before sitting down (you
could never be sure about bugs in those places) but
you have no idea how appreciative those people were
of her visits! It really brought some sunshine into
their drab lives. Of course she might be wrong (she
said), and I might not agree with her, but *she* believed
it was a Christian's duty to bring sunshine into
people's drab lives.

And so she went on. Incident after incident flooded
out, in all of which she was the central figure. There
was no bragging about it; she was not particularly
boastful. Most of what she said was quite trivial. No
one would have considered her wicked. She was just
wrapped up in herself. Her thoughts were running
round and round in one restricted circle. Though she
talked so volubly, I never heard her say a single
sentence which did not include a reference to herself.

At last I thought the time had come for me to introduce her to her new life. First I told her about heaven,
and her face glowed serenely. Then I told her about
hell, and she muttered, "My poor husband!" I said,

pointedly, that those in heaven think nothing of themselves, and dislike even referring to themselves in conversation. She said she was just like that, and how sorry she was for self-centered people, because they missed so much from life. And off she went again, with anecdote after anecdote to illustrate her complete unselfishness. As soon as I could get a word in, I went on to say that the angels are like empty vessels, completely empty of self, which the Lord fills with His own life. She said, "Ah yes! I am like that! How beautifully you have described my own case!"

This was getting ridiculous. I was beginning to be afraid to say anything at all, because whatever I said she immediately twisted round to herself. And gradually a more boastful element was entering in. Her references to her husband were becoming more bitter. Her physical charm was fading. Her tone of voice had become harsher, her speech more rapid and strident. Now she would not even listen when I tried to interrupt her. She just talked on and on, in an ever increasing crescendo, till I was afraid she might explode!

Stop her I must, if I was to do anything for her. So I decided to resort to extreme measures. There is a trick which we can perform when necessary. I opened a small channel between her mind and a certain region of hell, which resulted in her having a mild paralytic seizure. There was a sudden breath-taking silence. Her jaw stuck half open, and she gazed at me in horror. I knew she could hear everything I said, but could not move a muscle, let alone answer back.

"Don't be alarmed," I reassured her. "I shall hold you like this only for a few minutes while I talk to you, then I shall release you. Now please listen carefully. You are in a far more dangerous condition than

your husband. I have known many men who have been
driven to drink and adultery by the selfishness of their
wives; but almost always, when they have reached
this side and left their alcoholic, lusting physical bodies
in the grave, they have been only too pleased to make
a new beginning. But your obsession with self is more
interior — and it has been growing worse, even while
you have been speaking to me. Please try to appreciate
your extreme danger, and ask the Lord to have mercy
on you and save you, before it is too late. Now you can
have your speech back, and answer me how you like.''

Her mouth snapped shut. She shook herself, and
rose to her feet with great dignity. ''I am deeply
offended,'' she said. ''You have entirely misjudged
me. You do not understand me in the least. I have
been wasting my time talking to you. And apart from
incompetence, you have insulted me. I shall report you
to the authorities.'' And, still talking, she turned her
back to the Lord's glorious Sun, which was shining
so beautifully in the eastern sky, and set off walking
into her own shadow.

She was quite right, of course; I *am* incompetent
when it comes to pathological cases like hers. They
call me *Aqueduct,* because a little of the Lord's truth
trickles through me to those who are thirsty for it.
But if a person is not thirsty, I cannot help him. A
specialist is required. As soon as she had left me, I
tuned in to one of our senior men who had been an
eminent surgeon in your world. (How did I do it? Why,
I concentrated my thoughts upon him, and he immediately appeared before me; we talked together
until we had communicated fully, and then he disappeared.) This man has undertaken to give her a
clinical examination, to determine whether the cancer

has attacked and damaged her inmost Ruling Love. If it has, then I am afraid there is little hope for her. But, if she has any vital part unaffected by the disease, he will operate, and she may yet be saved. I earnestly pray to the Lord that it will be so.

Good-bye, and God bless you.

FIVE

GUARDIANS AND WARDS

Interview 5

GUARDIANS AND WARDS

This is Aqueduct speaking. Greetings, dear friend from the other side! I have just been talking to a friend of yours. You may not know him, but he has been going around with you for a long while and knows you intimately. He is, in fact, your Guardian Angel! He knows all about your visits here, and everything you have thought, said and written in connection with them. I must confess my curiosity was aroused, and I asked him to tell me some of your reactions, and what you think of the way we have been communicating. But he shut up like a clam; he would not reveal a thing! We angels cannot dissemble or tell lies, but we can refuse to communicate when confidences are involved. You need have no fear of indiscretions on his part.

The whole system by which the Lord cares for people on earth through the agency of guardian angels, centers and focuses in this Balance-Land, so perhaps I had better tell you something about it. As you know, the inhabitants of your world live here as to their spirits, though normally we cannot see them. (You are an exception!) They move around as tight little "spheres of influence" — bundles of thoughts and affections, which might be compared to static charges of electricity. Most of the time we are completely unaware of them; but if we concentrate our minds on them, we "feel" them passing among us, moving everywhere.

Broadly speaking, the Lord allocates to each and every man, woman and child on earth, two angels and two evil spirits. From this you can calculate that a very large proportion of the total inhabitants of both heaven and hell are occupied in this work. With the so-called "population explosion" in this New Age, it is becoming quite a problem to provide guardian angels and evil spirits for everyone. But the Lord has His own good reasons for increasing the population just now, and we can be sure He will not create new souls if He cannot also provide for their protection and needs.

I have never myself been a guardian angel; my work has always been with the new arrivals over here. It was not even granted to me to be a guardian for my beloved wife on earth, because I was too deeply involved with her personally, and I should probably have overwhelmed her. The entire success of the guardian-ward relationship depends on the guardian's respecting the free will of the ward. That is one reason why the Lord allows evil spirits to be present wherever there are angels: to preserve equilibrium.

Why two of each, you ask? Why not just one angel and one evil spirit? Well, I do not mean to speak too precisely or mathematically when dealing with spiritual influences, but the intention is that one angel shall present *Love to the Lord,* and the other *Love to the Neighbor,* while one evil spirit presents *Love of Self,* and the other *Love of the World.* Thus help is available from the point of view of each of the four possible love-motives. But in practice the ward generally accepts help from one only, inviting one of the angels or devils into the inner sanctum of his will as a counsellor, and leaving the others outside, where they stand by in case their services are required. Meanwhile, of course, they can get on with other work.

When an angel is informed by the Lord that he is to be a guardian to a certain person in your world, he seeks out that person's "sphere" here in Balance-Land, and attaches himself to it, entering fully into the person's thoughts, and even into his memory. Very soon he knows everything his ward is thinking or has ever thought. It even appears to the angel as if his ward's thoughts were his own thoughts; he identifies with him completely. But, with his greater experience and detached viewpoint, the angel is in a position to make suggestions and give advice, which he does in such a way that the ward imagines he has thought it all up for himself! To some extent also the angel can see through the ward's eyes into your world, so that he can give him premonitions of danger, and help him to react profitably to the external circumstances in which he finds himself.

There is one rule, however, that must be observed. The guardian must not enter into the ward's will or affections, except by invitation: that is to say, by attraction. The ward must have an inner desire to be motivated by the kind of love the angel represents; he must, as it were, open the door of his heart. Then the guardian angel can step right into the inner sanctum; his secret advice will be heard and heeded, and his influence for good will be enormous.

If he is rejected, and an evil spirit is invited in his place, he must leave at once. It is hard for him to stand by and see a vile devil or satan monopolizing his ward's will, tempting him and giving suggestions calculated to land him in hell, stirring up lust and jealousy, resentment and fear, and to be unable to do anything to prevent it! For it is obvious that, so long as an evil spirit is in the inner sanctum, the ward will not take much notice of the good advice of the angel. The evil spirit knows this, too, and sometimes gives a fiendish grimace of triumph, which makes the angel sad, because he knows that the evil spirit's sole aim is to enslave and destroy.

But, on the other hand, what joy and satisfaction when the ward can be led to realize his danger, and when he says, "Get thee behind me, Satan!" and drives out the evil spirit and admits the angel instead, and listens to him! Then the guardian can exercise himself to the utmost, giving love and peace and harmony and every spiritual grace.

Most guardian angels operate from their homes in heaven, which they can easily do since long-range communication is no problem in this spirit world. But if there is a crisis which requires concentrated attention, an angel will sometimes come down here into Balance-Land, to be nearer his ward. You can see them sitting under a tree, or in some secluded corner, head bowed, in deep abstraction; and you know they are loving and helping some struggling but hopeful soul on earth.

Unfortunately, however, you also see evil spirits around, trying to oppose them. Nor can anything be done to drive them away, so long as they are here by invitation of someone in your world — and well they know it!

My friend, I sense that you are still puzzled as to

why our loving Lord permits these evil spirits to compete with His own angels for a foot-hold in people's hearts and minds. I have already mentioned that a state of equilibrium must be maintained, for the sake of free will. Nothing becomes a man's own, unless he chooses it and adopts it freely, knowing the alternatives. Evil spirits are unable to do a man any harm, unless the man chooses freely to receive what they have to offer. But by the same token, angels are unable to do a man any *good,* unless he chooses to receive good from them, as of himself. This is why free will is so vitally important — even more important than freedom of action, though there must be some freedom of action if free will is not to be stifled.

Ironically, man needs to be tempted to do wrong in order to learn *not* to do wrong. It is true that we have been taught to pray, "Lead us not into temptation." (Yes! We repeat the Lord's Prayer over here, just as you do!) But that only presents the point of view of the one being tempted. He must try, as of himself but in the Lord's power, to drive the tempter out. That very effort strengthens him and builds him up. But what opportunity would there be to drive an evil spirit out, if he was never permitted to go in?

Evil spirits perform a real service without intending to do so. They show you that you have evils inherent in you, of which you would otherwise be unconscious. They are expert at doing this! They stir them up and make them active. You feel a strong urge to do various things which you know are wrong; or even to give way to fear, mistrust, or sicknesses of various kinds. Perhaps you yield to that urge, but afterwards feel disgusted with yourself. You repent, and the Lord forgives you, and you start again. Gradually you reach the state in which this particular evil has no further appeal; you are free of it.

If a man was never tempted by evil spirits, he would be like a hothouse plant, lacking in immunity and stamina. When he comes over here, after the death of his body, he would be totally unable to resist the influence of hell. Better to have your evils brought to your notice during your formative years in the physical world, when the development of resistance is comparatively easy for you. If a man discovers in your world that evil is unsatisfying and unsatisfactory, and therefore chooses good, then he becomes confirmed in good. When he comes over into Balance-Land, he sets forth to heaven willingly and without a backward glance.

The only case in which the Lord does not allow evil spirits to balance the influence of guardian angels, is with babies who are not yet old enough to choose. Angels from the very highest heaven are with them — angels "who always behold the face of our Father in heaven." That is why little babies have such an appeal, why it is such a moving experience to handle them, such a delight to caress them. They are little bits of heaven.

But, as the child begins to grow up and his own selfhood comes to the surface, the angels have to retire. Before leaving, they store up in a little closet or cache in the child's unconscious mind a supply of innocence and tenderness for use in later life. And so the battle begins. Evil spirits come and tempt him to do wrong; angels try to protect him by reminding him of the truths he is learning from God's Holy

Word, pointing to the unhappy results of evil experienced by himself and others, and, when necessary, drawing on that little store of innocence in the closet. This battle goes on daily throughout the whole of everybody's life, though most people are entirely unaware of it.

Tell them about it, will you?

And your own guardian angel has asked me to suggest to you that you should cooperate more with him. Of course I know nothing about it, since he did not confide in me, but I suspect from his attitude that you do not always listen to the good advice which he whispers into your thoughts, and that perhaps you sometimes throw him out and admit his rival from hell! Well, that is what he wants you to avoid doing in the future.

You will never be consciously aware of his presence, nor need you know who he is, for he is only an agent or representative of the Lord — "a fellow servant, one of your brethren that have the testimony of Jesus." But he greatly desires your salvation, and will help you in any steps you take towards a closer approach to our dear Lord, on whose behalf we are all working, and whose will it is that every one of us shall be happy in heaven to eternity.

It is for this reason that the Lord has arranged for all His children on both sides of the Veil to live together; and help one another; and has "given His angels charge over thee, to keep thee in all thy ways; they shall bear thee up in their hands, lest thou dash thy foot against a stone." And that is why, when the devils leave you for a season, "angels come and minister unto you."

I perceive, my friend, that your Guardian Angel is with you now, though you cannot see him. I will leave you to him.

Good-bye, and God bless you.

SIX

THE RAILROAD ACCIDENT

Interview 6

THE RAILROAD ACCIDENT

*This is Aqueduct speaking. Greetings, dear friend
from the other side!* It will be a pleasure to sit down
with you under this tree, and chat with you after a
heavy day's work. My colleagues and I have been helping people over from that big railroad accident which
took place near your home — maybe some of them are
friends or acquaintances of yours? Yes, two commuter
trains collided at a junction, and both jumped the
tracks. We were expecting it, as it had been foreseen,
and we had our whole staff ready.

I understand your newspapers are calling it a major
disaster and tragedy. It must seem like that to you,
but from our point of view things are rather different.
The whole purpose of your world is to provide and
prepare souls for life here, and every one of you will
come here eventually, so death itself is never a
tragedy, though it may involve sad separations. The
newspapers are also speaking of certain "miraculous"
escapes; but nothing which the Lord permits is more
miraculous than anything else, since His providence
is universal.

The actual situation is that the Lord takes everything into account in determining the hour of everyone's death: the man's own needs, his actions and the
actions of other people which impinge upon him, and
also the operation of the laws of mechanics and phy-

sics — which are God's laws for your world. If the greatest benefit, or the least harm, will accrue from any particular person's premature departure from your world, then that person will die young; otherwise, he will wait until his physical body is worn out with age.

Why yes, of course you are right to try to keep your friends in your world for as long as possible. A true instinct drives you to do this. And your loving concern will provide another element in the situation, which the Lord will take into account in determining when they will die. But having done your best, you can safely entrust your loved-ones to their heavenly Father's care, and not worry over the outcome.

Most of the souls who were precipitated from that railroad crash were unaware that anything crucial had happened, and it required a great deal of persuasion on our part to convince them that they had come into another world. Many of them were in the full flush of their business affairs, arrogant, anxious, earthbound. It was almost comical the way they kept glancing at imaginary wristwatches, and complaining that they would be late for their appointments! We tried to comfort them with the assurance that from now onwards their wristwatches would no longer be their bosses, and that their business appointments were of no great importance anyway. The transition, I fear, has been hard for most of them, since they were totally unprepared for it. How much easier it is for us and our clients, when a period of sickness has come first, to soften the hard outer crust, and break some of the mooring ropes which bind the mind to the earth life! Our easiest cases are old folks, who have grown "hard of hearing," whose eyes are dim, whose memory is confused. These slip over so sweetly, and awake so fresh and innocent — it is a real pleasure to receive them!

Those who die after a long terminal illness have an easy transition as a rule. And it is a strange fact of our experience, that when the illness has been particularly painful from a physical standpoint, the patient has often developed a wonderfully mature quality of mind. It is as if the discipline of the pain has strengthened them and removed their self-love, so that they can pass almost immediately up into heaven. Does this mean that sickness and suffering are part of the Lord's will for His children? No — a thousand times no! The Lord is an infinitely loving Father; His inflowing life brings with it nothing but radiant health and vitality. But our experience does show that good can triumph over evil, and that angelic qualities can, and often do, develop in a most adverse environment.

Do you know where disease comes from? Why, from those ugly and cruel spirits from hell whom one sometimes meets skulking around here in Balance-Land alongside your earth. Anyone who accidentally approaches them falls sick. I, myself, once went down with a high fever, and was off work for a week, because the wind blew towards me from one of them! Other evil spirits cause toothache and rheumatic pains, or cancer of various organs. And why are they up here in Balance-Land? Because someone on your side has fetched them up! They are here by invitation, so we just have to accept their presence. But at what a cost! Their poisonous influence affects the atmosphere of your world as well as ours, producing disease germs, bacteria, baccili — to say nothing of morbid growths and physical deformities. And, once these vile forms of death-giving life have gotten a bridge-head in your world, they breed and spread, so that innocent and guilty people suffer alike. However, though diseases can get a foothold on earth and spread, nobody is assaulted by an evil spirit unless he wills it; and always there are guardian angels at hand in case they are wanted.

You will see from all this why a right attitude of prayer, whether for oneself or for others, can have such a powerful healing influence. I verily believe that you people on earth could cure nearly all your ailments, if you prayed together in the Lord's strength. An even greater effect could be produced if every man and woman on earth were to shun evils as sins against God, saying, "Get thee behind me, satan!" There can be no doubt that these pestilential creatures would then have to decamp at once, and this Balance-Land would be cleared of their effluvia. Disease on your earth would disappear; your sick would recover, and soon your hospitals would be empty and your doctors would be without work. Why not suggest to your friends over there that they should try the experiment? Why do not the rulers of your nations undertake such a project? It would be more productive than some of the goals which I am told they pursue!

But the remarkable thing is (and here I am just lost in wonder and amazement) that the Lord uses the very evils which spring from the misuse of human free will, to help in your spiritual growth! He overrules them for good; they are transmuted into blessings. It is possible to derive spiritual benefits from pain, disappointment, failure and loss. When all goes well with a man, and his friends praise him and he gets everything he wants, then it is that self-love and greed flourish unchecked. But when things go badly, and people ignore or insult you, then your self-confidence can be broken down and you can be made humble — which is the best possible preparation for spiritual gain.

Poverty, hunger, accident, loss ... you can benefit from them all, if you react to them wisely. It is true, of course, that these troubles can have an injurious effect, making people bitter and resentful, so that they become spiritually harmed by them. But you can learn to be grateful for your misfortunes (as I am eternally grateful for those which came to me in my earth-life). You should welcome the stroke that falls on you. Then disaster itself will help you to climb the steep upward path to heaven.

The most terrible and tragic event in the whole history of the created universe, was ... the crucifixion of our beloved Lord Jesus Christ. I can hardly bear to think of it. ... Yet, God be praised! It served as the final phase of our Redemption!

Excuse me, my mind has been wandering. I see you are looking with recognition at that new arrival who is standing outside the Reception Hall gazing ecstatically toward the east. Do you know him? Ah yes, he was a neighbor of yours. He has been one of my best patients from the railroad accident. Please go to his widow and comfort her, and tell her she need not worry about him; he will soon be on his way to heaven. What did you say? He and his wife are separated — were on the point of divorce? That is amazing! I have examined his heart thoroughly, and I can assure you he loves his wife most tenderly, and is eagerly looking forward to the day she will be reunited with him here!

It is a perpetual source of astonishment to us, that you earth-people are so blind to one another's inner feelings. Those who love each other seem to hate, whereas those who hate each other seem to love. Yours is indeed a dark and confused world! How grateful you must all be that, through the Lord's mercy, the days of your life are numbered, and you can look forward with hope and confidence to your eventual release!

Good-bye, and God bless you.

SEVEN

A Trip to Hell

Interview 7

A TRIP TO HELL

This is Aqueduct speaking. Greetings, dear friend from the other side! I have just had a memorable experience which I should like to share with you. I have been on a trip to hell! For a long while it has seemed to me that a Receptionist could be of more help to the new arrivals from your world if he had actually seen for himself something of the conditions prevailing in the lower regions; and the opportunity came in the Lord's good time.

There has recently arrived a certain clergyman, an evangelical modernist of liberal views, who throughout his life on earth always denied the existence of hell. "How could a loving and merciful Creator punish his own children?" he would cry. I have named this man *Vindicator*, because he is always trying to vindicate the love and mercy of God — though one wonders why such vindication should be considered necessary! When he arrived here, and discovered that, despite the love and mercy of God, there is nevertheless a hell (in fact, there are many hells), he was at first incredulous and then profoundly shocked. I explained to him that hell is not a place of punishment, nor is anyone compelled to live there. This he could not believe: "for who," he said, "would go willingly to hell?"

As this was a matter of overwhelming importance

67

to him, and affected his whole attitude towards the
Lord as his heavenly Father, I asked one of my neighbors, who is a Guard in hell, to help me explain to
the Reverend Vindicator what the true position is.
This neighbor travels regularly to his place of employment in a flying carriage. "Why don't the two of
you come with me tomorrow," he said, "and see for
yourselves?"

Normally, to get to a distant place, we concentrate
our thoughts on where we want to go, give the word
of command, and the strength of our determination
carries us speedily to our destination. Yes, we fly like
the birds; but, as you see, we have no wings. (Angels
with wings! How absurd! We should not be human
beings but monstrosities!) Actually I fly to this Middle Region every morning from my home in the foothills of heaven, and back again each evening when
my day's work is done. It is a pleasant and relaxing
experience. But to get to hell is another thing altogether. How could anyone concentrate his thoughts
on a region so utterly alien to his own? So my friend
the Guard travels in a flying carriage. There are many
kinds available. The prophets of old called them
"chariots of fire," for *chariot* was the only word they
knew to indicate a moving vehicle. Today you would
probably call them aircraft, or even space modules!
To travel to hell is rather like visiting another planet.

We were given what you would call space suits, to
enable us to live in the poisonous atmosphere, and
endure the stenches which I am told are frightful, and
to protect us from the dead heat or dead cold of those
nether regions, and from the destructive rays emanat-
ing from the inhabitants; and also, it was explained,

to protect *them* from *us!* These suits are practically invisible, and do not hamper one's movements to any extent.

Our flying carriage rose into the air, and we set off floating towards the west, over the escarpment of the Middle Region which drops away like a precipice. Soon the sun disappeared, and night closed around us. I began to feel nervous and homesick, and it required a definite effort of prayer before I felt the Lord's presence with me again. The Reverend Vindicator seemed quite scared, so we all prayed together, and soon a soft glow of light filled the carriage and we knew we were safe. Looking out through the windows, we could see straggling cities far below us. Some of them seemed to be on fire, with flames leaping into the air and billows of smoke. Suddenly, a volcano erupted beneath us; a trail of molten lava moved down into a lake, from which rose clouds of steam.

"These conflagrations and eruptions are hell fire," commented our guide. "They produce a kind of light which takes the place of the sun for them."

I asked what sort of hell we were going to, for I knew there were hells of many different kinds: frozen hells, where cold-blooded people live; tropical jungle hells, where people's lusts and passions are forever inflamed; hot desert hells, where the life of the inhabitants is completely sterile; stormy hells, flooded hells, dry hells. I knew some hells were thickly populated, while in others the inhabitants live an almost solitary existence. As always in this spirit world, the environment is a reflection of the inner state of the people who live there.

"We are not going far," our guide explained. "The hell where I work is not very deep down, and the climate is fairly temperate, as in Balance-Land. My folk there believe they are still in the natural world, for they cannot rise to a conception of anything spiritual; and so, by hallucination and fantasy, they produce all the things they enjoyed in the old life. They drink whiskey and quarrel and rob one another, just as they used to do. And the whole area is a squalid slum."

"Did they live in slums on earth?" I asked him.

"Not necessarily," he said. "Many did; others were from the upper crust, children of the wealthy. But they all had the slum mentality."

I inquired whether there were any better-class neighborhoods in hell. He told us there were many such, especially towards the north, where the inhabitants are crazy for property and possessions. They live in great pomp and extravagance, in flamboyant homes like palaces, with Greek pillars and marble statues; or in enormous battlemented castles. The rooms are so full of furniture and ornaments and art treasures and knick-knacks that you can hardly find space enough to stand in. These people accumulate such quantities of possessions that they have to build endless annexes and outhouses to contain them. They cling to every article, however useless, as if their lives depended on it. They would rather undergo torture than yield up a single item, and live in a continual torment of fear lest they should be robbed. Many of them were from the poorest of the poor on earth, but not all. Again, it is a question of mentality. He told us we might visit one of these affluent hells some other time, but today we were bound for the slum areas, where the inhabitants did not care a rap for their surroundings.

As we were talking, I suddenly felt that the flying carriage was beginning to descend. Down we came, and landed gently in front of a large building, which seemed to be the administration offices. The door of our vehicle opened, and we stepped out. Our eyes soon became accustomed to the dim light, and with a little practice we could breathe and walk about quite freely.

Behind the administration building stretched a high fence of barbed wire.

"A concentration camp!" muttered my friend Vindicator, fingering the spikes.

The Guard unlocked a small gate in the fence, and let us through. We followed him along a narrow alley between shanties with chimneys belching smoke, and shacks made of old bedsteads and burlap. Soon we were engulfed in a maze of lanes between dilapidated tenement buildings. Garbage and filth lay everywhere. Hostile faces peered out at us from doors and broken windows.

"What puzzles me," said Vindicator, "is how a God of love and mercy could make people live in a place like this." (He jumped back to avoid a pailful of refuse that was flung out of an open door.)

"On the contrary," answered the Guard. "I and my associates are trying to move the people out, so as to clear the site for rebuilding. The whole area inside the fence is condemned property. We take them away, a few at a time, to a place where they can train to become respectable citizens. But they are so cunning! Most of them escape and come back here. They climb in through the barbed wire, even tearing their flesh in their eagerness.''

"So the barbed wire fence is to keep people *out,* not keep them *in*?'' exclaimed our clerical friend, with dawning comprehension.

"Assuredly,'' said the Guard.

"So God does not compel these people to live here?'' persisted Vindicator.

"Indeed no,'' answered the Guard. "Hell is illegal, from start to finish.''

Hell is illegal! There was a pause while the implications of this remark sank in. Then suddenly my friend drew back with horror, and pointed to a small group of people ahead of us. "See!'' he cried, "Those poor wretches are being burned to death! They are writhing in fire!''

The Guard smiled. "But don't you see?'' he explained. "The fire is coming out of themselves! It is a projection of their lusts and passions.''

Yes, we could see it now. Some were staring at us fiercely, with fire flickering from their hostile eyes, and smoke belching from their snarling mouths. Others were running hither and thither, deliberately fanning their burning clothes. An eruption of smoke and cinders drew our attention to two men fighting savagely with sticks. Hell fire again.

Out of the corner of our eyes we could see scrawny animals — wolves, hyenas or jackals — eating the garbage or just lurking around; when we looked straight at them, they ran away. It was impossible to tell whether they were real animals, or human beings that resembled animals.

Suddenly a shriek rent the air, then another and

another. My companion's face blanched, and he clutched my arm. "It's the torture," he muttered. "In God's name, we must stop it." He dashed off in the direction of the cries, the Guard and I following as quickly as we could. We reached the house, and Vindicator wrenched open the door.

We were in a squalid room with cracks in the walls. A smoking kerosene lamp hung from a nail. The table was littered with an accumulation of bottles and glasses, pots and dishes and plates and remains of food. The shrieks came from a wild-looking woman in a soiled and torn dress. She had apparently hit her husband with a poker, and blood was dripping from his head. He had now caught her by the throat, and was forcing her down, down to the ground. In a few moments he must surely have throttled her, but, surprised by our sudden entry, he let her go. She sprang to her feet, and faced not *him* but *us* — looking more like a tiger than a human being.

"What do you want?" she snarled. "This is a private house, isn't it? Can't we do what we like in our own home? We want no policemen spying here." She seized the frying pan from the stove and flung it at Vindicator, missing his head by inches. We forcibly drew him out and shut the door. In a few minutes the screams began again.

"Don't worry," said the Guard. "This is all under control. Those two are allowed to punish each other in that way, because only thus can their love of domination be kept within reasonable bounds. They are already better than they used to be, thank God."

Vindicator was lost in thought as we continued on our way. "My problem," he said, "is a theological one. Did not Christ redeem these people by His passion on the cross? Has not the Father forgiven them, for Christ's sake? Can they not go free?''

"You had better tell them that," said the Guard with a smile.

We approached a large ramshackle building which looked like a dance hall, and slipped inside through a door marked "Bar." People were singing bawdy songs, which were interrupted by idiotic, mirthless laughter. A scantily dressed female was serving liquor. She took a glass to a prosperous looking gentleman slumped on a chair. He was too drunk to notice. She looked at him defiantly and without shame, then slipped her hand into his breast pocket and drew out his bulging wallet. Someone snatched it away from her; she rapped his hand and he dropped it. Someone else seized it, and immediately there was an uproar, everybody punching, biting and kicking everybody else. Oblivious of the madhouse scene, half-a-dozen men and women sat along the wall smoking some kind of dope; they looked scarcely alive.

The Reverend Vindicator boldly clapped his hands and called for attention. The fighting ceased abruptly, and all except the inebriated turned menacingly towards him. "I beseech you, my beloved brethren," he pleaded, "leave this fearful place! Your sins have been forgiven you. The Son of God has redeemed you. He died for you on Calvary Hill. You need not stay here any longer. The gate will be unlocked for you. You may go!"

"Go?" snarled one of the guests. "What is he talking about? We've paid our money, haven't we? On what authority is he telling us to go?"

"In the Name of our Lord Jesus Christ," pronounced the Reverend Vindicator.

There was an uneasy silence, and some of the guests edged away. "Don't say that Name again!" whispered one of them, nervously. Then, recovering his self-assurance: "We know all about the One you mentioned. But even He can't force us out of hell. It would be interfering with our freedom. He respects our freedom, doesn't He? A preacher fellow once told me He died to make us free!"

I was horrified. This was going too far. The Guard raised his hand. There was a rumble of thunder, followed by a gust of wind which shook the building to its foundation. The wind increased in force; the walls became wisps of rag, then cobwebs, then vapor, and soon it had all blown away. People were running frantically in all directions, seeking cover. When at last the gale subsided, we were alone.

Back in the administration building, and afterwards in the flying carriage, the Guard explained to us that there is, indeed, frightful suffering in hell. Punishment is administered by the evil spirits themselves, who enjoy nothing better than to torture one another. It is permitted by the Lord, if and when He perceives that some good can come from it. Sadly enough, punishment is often the only force which can break and reduce a spirit's evil desires sufficiently to enable him to live with others in some sort of ordered society. Once anyone has entered the spirit world, his evil ruling love cannot be changed; it can only be battered down by fear and pain.

Oh, dear friend, this is indeed a dreadful topic, one which I wish I could spare you. Could you not give an earnest warning to your readers over there? Impress upon them how vitally important it is for them to overcome their evil tendencies while they are still living in the formative world, the world where changes can be made with comparative ease! Pride, hatred, contempt of others, deceit, adultery, self-abuse by drink or drugs, envy, covetousness . . . shun these like hell itself, which they are! Root them out, while there is yet time; for insofar as these evils are still ruling you when you come over here, you will be abject slaves to eternity!

Good-bye, and God bless you.

EIGHT

RESUSCITATION

RESUSCITATION

This is Aqueduct speaking. Greetings, dear friend from the other side! I understand you would like to know a little more about the actual process of resuscitation, by which your "dead" awake to their spiritual life. Why, of course, I can describe it for you in some detail, since it is happening here all the time!

It takes place in one of the inner rooms of the Reception Building, rooms which resemble delivery rooms in your maternity hospitals on earth. Waking up in this world is similar in many respects to being born. The main difference is that with us there is no mother: your world itself is the common "mother" of us all. Life in your world is, as it were, the *gestation* for life over here, and you are only fully formed when you leave your world and enter eternity.

There are quite a number of Waking-Up Places like ours scattered throughout Balance-Land. It is of very little importance whether the dying enter this world through one or through another; all adjustments are made afterwards, as the ruling love begins to assert itself. The main consideration is that he should feel *at home,* that there should be as little shock as possible in connection with the crossing. If a man favors some particular city, he is allowed to cross over into the region of Balance-Land corresponding to that city, so that he will be comfortable when he wakes up. Our Waking-Up Place here is moderately rural, as you see. Actually it corresponds to your own region of the world; that is why you are here, and why most of your friends and neighbors come over through us.

When someone in your world is about to die, the Lord informs his guardian angels, who make all the necessary arrangements. If he is to come to us, we are informed, and a room is prepared for him. We have just as many rooms as we need. If another is required, it automatically appears; if any are not needed, they vanish. That is the normal way with rooms and furniture and such-like objects in this spirit world.

I, myself, am not qualified to be in attendance at a resuscitation; only senior receptionists are employed in this crucial work. I am not even permitted to approach closely until the body has awakened. But I have watched the procedure many times by "distant vision" — a kind of spiritual television, so I am fairly familiar with it.

The patient appears first as just a wraith or ghost lying on a couch, with, perhaps, other wraiths around him, who are the mourners at his bedside. As he begins to contemplate the prospect of death, his body becomes more solid and substantial.

Two of our most senior receptionists then enter the room and sit, one at the head and one at the foot. Between them they produce such a powerful sphere of love to the Lord that no lesser spirits can approach, let alone evil spirits from hell. This sphere gives off a kind of aromatic perfume, which I understand is sometimes actually smelt by the mourners on your side, if their spiritual senses are keen.

The angel at the head feels the patient's heart. Its pulse is light and erratic, which indicates that it is no longer producing heartbeats in the physical body. The lung movements also are shallow. The angel now gazes with fixed concentration into the patient's face. This drives out his thoughts, and the angel takes over the control of his mind, with the result that the patient gradually loses consciousness. As soon as the angel can see himself reflected in the patient's face, and the reflection comes into focus, he knows the man is "dead" and ready for the actual resuscitation.

The Lord, Himself, now takes over. Whenever possible, the Lord acts through angels or men, but in the resuscitation of the dead He works alone. It is a kind of withdrawal of the spirit from every organ, fibre and cell of the physical body, and in particular from the brain with all its nerve ends, and the re-connection of them so that the man's senses will thenceforth operate in and through his spiritual body instead of his physical. The physical body is now dead and useless, like the sloughed skin of a snake. It can be disposed of in any way you people wish, for it will never be required again.

After the withdrawal is complete, the man's spiritual body on the bed becomes solid and substantial, like our own. He is still unconscious, for the angel is still gazing fixedly into his face; but his heartbeats become normal and his full breathing is resumed. The operation being completed, the angel at last withdraws his anaesthetic gaze, and the patient gradually regains consciousness, but ON THIS SIDE OF THE VEIL. At first he believes he is still in his bed on earth, perhaps awaking from a pleasant dreamless sleep. He has not yet opened his eyes, but he feels the sphere of the angels. This at first is sweet to him, but it very soon becomes unpleasantly intense, even overpowering. Perceiving this, the senior angels courteously retire, and are replaced by two others from a lower heaven with whom the patient can feel more at ease.

These set to work at once to get his senses operating again, especially the sense of sight. It seems to the waking person (they have often told me afterwards) as if a membrane was being peeled off from the left eye towards the bridge of the nose, letting in a dim light — the color being different with various individuals. Then another membrane seems to be rolled off from the whole face, giving full vision. The angels are extremely careful that only loving thoughts shall occupy the mind until the patient is fully awake; this is especially important if the patient had been suffering great pain and was feeling resentful or self-pitying.

The new arrival now jumps from the couch, tests himself all over, and finds he is in perfect condition. This surprises him if he was previously in a sick bed; but he is even more surprised, as a rule, when he is informed that he is a spirit! In appearance his body resembles what it was before: he is an old man, perhaps, with white hair and a beard. He gazes around the room, and sees the same objects that were in his bedroom when he "died." (We cannot see them, but he can.) But where, he asks, are his loved ones who were with him so recently? And who are these new friends who are with him now? He looks at them carefully. If he feels attracted to them, they remain with him; but more commonly, as his former state of life returns, he begins to feel uncomfortable in their presence, and so they depart, and a few of us junior receptionists take over. What happens after that I have explained to you in some of our former interviews.

You ask whether there is any difference in the process of resuscitation if the physical body has been blown to bits in an explosion. Here the spirit is left, as it were, in total suspension. But from our point of view things are much the same, for the spiritual body is potentially complete even though the physical body has disappeared. The Lord does not have to draw the spirit out, but He has to connect up the senses with the spiritual nerve ends as before. There is not much difference really. How long does resuscitation take? Ah, that is a question I cannot answer, as we have no yardstick for measuring time in this world. Someone has mentioned *three days,* which may be about right. In the case of our Lord Jesus Christ when He "died" on your earth, only one day and a half intervened between His loss of consciousness on the cross on Good Friday, and His resurrection from the sepulchre early on Easter Sunday morning. But that Event was unique.

Guardian angels sometimes tell us that their wards are attending the burial service of some loved one who has just been resuscitated; that is as far as we can go from the point of view of dating. They inform the new arrival: "Your funeral is now being conducted, and a lot of complimentary things are being said about you (we hope they are true!) and everybody is weeping!" To which the new arrival generally retorts with indignation: "But I am alive! How can anyone say I am dead?"

Speaking for myself, I cannot remember anything at all about my resuscitation, any more than a child can recollect anything of his birth. Perhaps in your case you will remember more, because you will know what to expect and will be prepared to follow the process through. But I am sure that when the angel gazes into your face, you will lose consciousness completely, just as everybody else does!

It has sometimes occurred to me to wonder what would happen in the case of a saint who had developed such a high degree of love to the Lord during his life on earth that he could receive the senior receptionist's gaze and return it like a brother. Would his transition be conscious — a mere stepping over, as it were, from one world into another? Perhaps the time will come when many people will regenerate so far in your world that they will be able to step over like that. But your modern western culture is not designed to produce saints. I doubt whether *you* are one, anyway! Nevertheless, my friend, take heart! You can rest assured that your resuscitation, when it comes, will be completely painless. Your transition will be a happy one, and will introduce you to just the kind of life you would be living now, if you could!

Good-bye, and God bless you.

NINE

PREDESTINATION VERSUS FREEDOM

PREDESTINATION *vs.* FREEDOM

This is Aqueduct speaking. Greetings, dear friend from the other side! We have just had an interesting debate between two clergymen on the subject of "Predestination versus Human Freedom." I had previously heard these two men arguing together on the lawn, and since they seemed well matched and the subject was a vital one, I suggested we should stage a public debate. We prepared our largest auditorium and advertized it well, so that about a thousand people were present.

The first speaker mounted the platform and presented his case. He believed in "Predestination," so I will call him "Reverend Predestination." God is omniscient, he maintained, and so God sees into the future and knows exactly where every person will finally be, in heaven or in hell. "This means," he said, "that the future is *fixed,* and every man's life is predetermined from birth to death and beyond. Therefore," he said, "man has no freedom of action, nor even freedom of thought since his thoughts are also fixed."

The other speaker now mounted the platform. He took the opposite position, and so I will call him "Reverend Freedom." "Man is a free agent," he maintained. "Man has complete freedom of will and choice, and partial freedom of action. Therefore God cannot foresee the future, except in the sense that God can estimate that certain results would follow from a certain action if the man chose to perform that action." The Reverend Freedom conceded that God *could* be omniscient, but in fact God has deliberately given man the power of free choice. "And so," said Reverend Freedom, "God obviously cannot see beyond any point at which man exercises his freedom." In other words, God cannot see beyond the present moment, for man might suddenly assert himself at this moment and do something unpredictable. "If my friend is right in maintaining that man cannot act in freedom," the Reverend Freedom continued, "then he must tell us who introduced evil into the world? If not man, then it must have been God. This is blasphemy!"

The audience applauded, lights flashed, and for a while the "Human Freedom" point of view prevailed. But soon opinions changed again, for the Reverend Predestination showed that if we restrict God's vision to the past and present, and deny Him any knowledge of the future, we are making Him a limited creature like ourselves, which itself is blasphemy. How could God's Providence operate, he asked, if God's wisdom were so circumscribed? Does not such a view deny the Providence of God?

To this the Reverend Freedom retorted: "Sir, it is *you* who are making nonsense of the Providence of God! What kind of a loving God is this, Who allows certain people to be born, knowing that they are lost souls who will spend eternity in hell? What kind of Providence is this, that elects and favors some but damns others?"

Again the audience applauded and the lights flashed. The Reverend Predestination seemed somewhat shaken. "No, my friend," he protested, "you misunderstand me! God damns nobody. I will admit that the wicked damn themselves. I will even concede that God does not predestine anybody to hell. But He *foresees* that they will go to hell. He foresees the final state of everyone, whether it is in heaven or hell."

"That is much better," said the Reverend Freedom. "Yet still I do not agree with you. Is there any real difference between foresight and predestination? If a man's future is foreseen by God, then it is fixed and unalterable. In that case, is it not predestined?"

And so the two contestants went from one extreme to the other. In the end there was deadlock, and one of the angel receptionists was asked to resolve the dilemma. He mounted the platform and stood between the two clergymen, with a hand laid affectionately on each. The auditorium, which during the debate had been alternately dark and light in response to the feelings of the audience, now brightened into a roseate glow, and soft music began to sound.

"Both our dear friends are right in their main statements," said the angel. "It is indeed true that God is omniscient. He has absolute foresight, and can see everything from eternity to eternity. He knows where each and every soul will make his or her final abode, in heaven or in hell." (The audience applauded, and the Reverend Predestination looked pleased and nodded.) "And it is undeniable," continued the angel, "that man has absolute freedom of choice, and freedom of action in certain areas. Evil and hell have arisen from man's misuse of this freedom."

There was another burst of applause. The two contestants shook hands and embraced each other. Then,
looking at the angel with a growing bewilderment,
they said, "But sir! The two statements are contra-
dictory! How can they both be true?"

There was an expectant silence in the vast auditorium, as the angel began to expound the concept of
time in relation to eternity, of "God-Immanent" and
"God-Transcendent," of "God Within His Creation"
and "God Outside and Above it." I wish you could
have heard him, dear friend from the other side, as I
am unable to present the subject as wonderfully as
he did.

Time is an enigma. We know nothing of measurable
time in this spirit world: what seems like a hundred
years to one may be only a few minutes to another.
In your world, however, for the sake of your progres-
sive growth and regeneration, the Lord has given you
a kind of corridor of time, through which you must all
move at a fixed and measurable speed. It is like a
moving belt such as you use in your factories. All the
inhabitants of your earth-planet are moving through
the dimension of time together at the same speed. You
encounter situations simultaneously, which are plan-
ned by Providence to give you the maximum opportunity for character formation and development. Other
planets also have time, arranged for the benefit of
their inhabitants, but it is different from yours. It
varies, I believe, according to the planet's speed of
movement through space: the planet which is moving
fastest has the slowest time system. Theoretically it
would be possible for a planet to travel so fast that

its time would go into reverse; but this the Lord will not allow.*

Time, then, is a local phenomenon, not at all built into the structure of the universe. In vast areas of open space, there is no time. You cannot say that "now" with you is the same as "now" with a human being on some other planet. It becomes absurd, therefore, to maintain that the Creator is restricted in His omniscience by time, that He cannot see beyond the moment we call "now." He is infinitely outside and above all those little corridors of time which He has laid out for the use of His creatures. He is transcendent, and can look down upon any point of the scheme, from an eternal past to an eternal future.

The basic error of the predestinationist is to suppose that the Lord sees the future *from the present,* whereas in fact He sees the future *from the future.* If it were possible to see the future from the present, then man would indeed have no freewill! That would indeed be predestination! But even God cannot do that. The future does not lie latent in the present and, even by knowing all there is to know about the present, God cannot foretell the future from it. For we make the future as we go along, by the exercise of our freedom of choice.

What the Lord can do, and does do, is to see the future from the future. He "goes into the future" and sees what actually will happen (or what actually does happen). He sees us exercising our freewill, and making our choices, one by one. Oh yes, He can watch events taking place in the future just as easily as He

---

* Aqueduct is evidently referring to the speed of light, 186,000 miles per second.

can watch them taking place in the present, and He can cooperate with us equally well there as here. He can see the whole of your life spread out before you, as you are going to make it, with your doubts and struggles, and final decisions and actions; and He can help you at every point. He can watch you choosing your final home in heaven or hell, and settling down there. All this is in the future, of course; it has not yet taken place in your time corridor, and it largely rests with you how it will take place. It is neither predetermined nor predestined. Yet the Lord knows how it will be, simply because He can slip forward into the future and see it. Thus, foresight is entirely different from predestination, and has nothing in common with it.

I have said that the Lord cooperates with man, and we know from personal experience that He does do this. He can, because, besides being transcendent, He is also immanent. He is with us, working by our side, involved in all the minute particulars of our everyday life, trying to bend the evil towards good, or at any rate to a lesser evil, and trying to make the good ever better. "God Immanent" is within time, whereas "God Transcendent" is outside and above time; and if God were not both Immanent and Transcendent, how could He help us?

I cannot leave the subject without referring to the Reverend Freedom's criticism, that if God foresees the future, He is in effect committing the cruelty of allowing people to be born who He knows will be damned in hell. What possible alternative is there? Should God destroy at birth those He foresees will end up in hell? But, if He destroyed them at birth, they would not end up in hell, so how could He foresee them in hell? (He only foresees what actually *does* take place, not what *would* take place *if* . . . .) To destroy an evil man at any time, right up to his entry into hell, would be to deprive him of the opportunity to make an eleventh-hour conversion and go to heaven instead.

Anyway, the devils and satans themselves would strongly resent any suggestion that God should have destroyed them "to save them from being damned in hell." They are in hell because they want to be in hell, and it is of the Lord's mercy and grace that they are permitted to live in that hellish way. The Lord loves them dearly, though He grieves for them. He would much rather have them where they want to be, even in hell, than have them somewhere where they do not want to be, even in heaven. And He would much rather have them in hell than not have them at all.

The Lord, then, can and does foresee the future. But, by the same token, man must not be permitted to do so, as foresight would destroy his freedom of action, which is an essential part of the creative process. How could you possibly choose in freedom, if you knew beforehand how you were going to choose? Therefore, prophecies and auguries of an unambiguous character, which would affect people's behavior, are forbidden.

We on this side are sometimes permitted to see into the future, if our work requires it. I have been allowed to, on occasion, so I can assure you that the future is there to be seen! But the one thing I most desire to foresee, is withheld from me. I should like to know when my beloved wife will join me here. But, if I knew this, I would undoubtedly reveal it to her, and that would destroy her freewill. So we must all just wait for that magic web, woven of the Lord's Providence and man's free choices, to unroll, meanwhile being patient in the knowledge that eternity lies before us.

Good-bye, and God bless you.

TEN

"Unto Him That Hath ..."

Interview 10

"UNTO HIM THAT HATH ... "

This is Aqueduct speaking. Greetings, dear friend from the other side! You do not appear to have been very successful, yet, in spreading a knowledge of the spiritual world among your earth folk, for many of them still arrive here with fantastic notions of what heaven is like. Some base their ideas of angels on the symbolic figures seen by the prophets in their visions and mentioned in the Bible: seraphs with six wings, cherubs with wheels and burning coals; a lion with eagle's wings and a man's heart; a bear with ribs in its mouth; a beast with iron teeth and ten horns; a calf with wings full of eyes; creatures with four faces. Yes, we do see such objects here. They are used in our teaching courses, and we learn a great deal from them by the language of symbolism. But, my friend: to meet one of these and mistake it for an angel ... !

As far as possible, we let people have what they expect. This is one of our principal training techniques. It is necessary to experience a thing to understand it properly. For example, if a new arrival thinks as many do, that angels sit on clouds playing harps, he is instantly given a small portable harp and is hoisted up onto a cloud in the sky, where he has to sit and strum on his instrument until he grows tired of it and begs to be allowed to return to normal life. He is usually careful not to mention the subjects of harps again!

Some people come over here with the belief that heaven consists of eternal rest. They envisage flowery banks where they will recline at ease and eat fruit out of golden platters. It is done! Nothing easier! And there they lie on beds of roses, sucking grapes and feeling intolerably bored. Males from the Moslem religion usually expect to have troupes of dancing girls, since that pleasure has been promised them in some of their holy books; and certain males from your part of the world also hope for something of the kind. Well, they are given all they want; but, after an eternity or two, how stale and flat it becomes! And what a relief when we let them out and give them something useful to do!

One shy and modest new arrival said he had always believed the Biblical statement that in heaven he would sit on a throne and judge the twelve tribes of Israel. This was immediately arranged for him. Liveried servants were provided, to be at his beck and call, and twelve groups of Israelites were brought in for judgment. Of course he had no idea what to do about them, or what judgments he ought to make, and was soon weary of the whole thing. It was then explained to him that the "tribes of Israel" whom he must govern were the elements within his own nature.

These little experiments prepare our new arrivals for the concept of heaven as a place of great human activity, where everybody exercises his gifts creatively in the service of others. Heaven is a kingdom of uses.

At various points between here and the foothills of heaven are schools and training establishments of

various kinds, where you can learn everything you
need to know. You can take courses in the Word of
God, which are wonderful and exciting, as I remember
from my own early days here. Then there are fasci-
nating lectures in Christian doctrine. Most people,
even from Christian lands, seem to have very little
knowledge of the truths of religion. Some have confirmed themselves in falsities which have to be un-
learned before any progress can be made. For example,
some have the idea that there are three separate
Persons in the Godhead, whom they call Father, Son,
and Holy Ghost. So long as they divide up the Holy
Trinity in this way, they cannot enter heaven, for
there is only One God in heaven. He is the Lord Jesus
Christ, who Himself declared, after His Resurrection,
"All power is given unto Me in heaven and in earth."
The Holy Trinity resides solely in Him. ("In Him
dwelleth all the fulness of the Godhead bodily.") The
Father is His infinite Divine Soul. The *Son* is the
Humanity which grew up during His life on your
earth, and which He afterwards glorified by uniting
it with His Soul. The *Holy Ghost* or *Holy Spirit* is
His outpouring Divine Life. To pray to the Father
for the sake of the Son, or as a Being separate from
the Son, is to cut God into two. Such prayers are forbidden here. We simply pray to the glorified Lord
Jesus Christ.

Full opportunities are given in these classes for
questions and discussion and, whenever convenient,
debates are arranged, and prizes are given to the
speakers whose opinions approximate most closely to
the truth. In addition to the more formal courses,
there are lessons for developing the faculty of *concentration,* without which one cannot pray satisfactorily

for any period of time. Help also is given in the art of *relaxation*, which enables one to open oneself to the inflow of divine life.

Everybody learns to the full capacity of his love — no more and no less. Love is like a sponge which sucks up just enough knowledge to fill it, but never more than that amount. The purpose of the training here in Balance-Land is to match each new arrival's goodness with its appropriate truth. He who comes here with much goodness (that is to say, much love for the Lord and for other people) receives a proportionately large amount of truth; he is our best student, irrespective of whether in your world he was an ignoramus or a college professor. Whereas, he who comes here with no goodness in his heart (no love of the Lord or of other people) learns nothing, and even forgets what he knew. "Unto him that hath, is given; and from him that hath not, is taken away."

As our students move forward from place to place, always in the direction of the mountains, they are occasionally joined by evil spirits, who secretly emerge from caves or from holes concealed by rocks, which are actually connected with hell by subterranean passages. These spirits are very subtle, and disguise themselves as angels of light sent by God to guide the newcomers to heaven. By flattery they insinuate themselves into the students' confidence, and implant doubts in their minds. They stir up and revive the selfhood, that old *ego* which has been dropping into the background during training, and induce an almost overpowering desire to be indignant, resentful, jealous, and self-righteous; to turn away from the Lord, and be contemptuous of others. If these evil spirits succeed in their hellish designs, the student has to go right

back to the beginning and start all over again. Usually, however, conscience prevails; the Lord's help is
sought, and the tempters are sent packing. Every
time this happens, a student's conscience becomes
stronger, and the force of his *ego* weakens, until he is
fully reborn as a child of God. Thus, the evil spirits,
from the very worst of motives, actually help in our
students' education!

As you will see, training for heaven is arduous and
often takes a long while, with many reverses. By con-
trast, how easy it is for the evil to go to hell! No
training is necessary; they just do what comes
naturally. Truth is an embarrassment to them, so they
simply reject all the truth they have ever known, and
in its place fabricate falsities which will justify and
excuse their evil ways.

A learned and successful preacher came over here
the other day. One could see immediately that he was
a religious hypocrite by his unctuous manner and his
forceful way of getting other people to agree with
him. He asked us for a cathedral, so we gave him one
at once, and we even filled it for him with an over-
flowing congregation. (You realize, of course, that this
was pure fantasy. The buildings, objects and robots
we produce for teaching purposes have no real existence, and are seen only by the people concerned.) The
reverend doctor preached a 'powerful and eloquent
sermon about faith and seemed gratified when the
congregation rose to its feet and applauded!

Our friend preached regularly in his cathedral for
several weeks, and we began to notice that a change
was taking place in his emphasis. Two points were
coming more and more to the forefront of his teaching:
firstly, that it did not matter what you did, or how

evil you were, so long as you had faith; and secondly, that you must agree with and admire the reverend doctor!

After a while he left us and moved further on to the west, where he said he felt he would get a better following. I watched him from time to time on the spiritual television, as he approached the borders of hell. Then came the crash. He was in a large church, preaching very dramatically about himself, when a youth in the congregation shouted something back at him. The preacher was furious and, losing his temper, threw his Bible at the boy's head. Immediately there was pandemonium, everybody hitting and throwing things at everybody else, so that the church building burst into flame, and the congregation scattered, running for their lives and leaping over the escarpment into hell. The reverend doctor was lost in the crowd, and I have not heard of him since. (By the way, it turned out that the book he had thrown at the young man's head was not a Bible at all, but the preacher's own autobiography, bound up to look like a Bible.)

Your world and our world differ in this, that true beliefs are much more important with you than with us. In your society, prejudices and false opinions can lead good-living religious people into wars, heresy hunts, crusades, racial discrimination, and all kinds of abuse. To make your world like heaven, society must accept the truths of heavenly life and obey the laws of heaven. That is why the Lord has revealed so much truth to your world. But when an individual comes over here, the important thing is not what he believes but what he loves and how he loves. A man's love is the one thing he brings with him after the death of his physical body, and he keeps it to eternity. A man's love is himself.

False beliefs are quickly dealt with and corrected here in Balance-Land, if the love is good. True beliefs, on the other hand, are even more quickly dispersed and dropped if the love is bad. That is why, when our Lord Jesus Christ was asked what were the main teachings of the new religion He was introducing into the world, He said nothing about its teachings. Instead, what did He say? "Thou shalt *love* the Lord thy God with all thy heart, soul, mind and strength; and thou shalt *love* thy neighbor as thyself. For, unto everyone that hath (love), to him shall be given, and he shall have abundance; but from him that hath not (love), shall be taken away, even that which he hath."

Before we separate, I feel I should say just a word about old age, since the majority of our new arrivals are elderly. But you must understand that old age is only a physical condition. Old people, if they are good at heart, grow progressively younger as they undergo their training here, and by the time they reach heaven they are in the springtime of perfect youth, but with the wisdom of maturity stamped on their features. The longer they reside in heaven, the more perfect that springtime becomes, with increase in vitality and freshness according to the development of their love and wisdom. We have a saying in these parts: "To grow old in heaven is to grow young." So you need not worry about your gray hairs!

Good-bye, and God bless you.

ELEVEN

THE BIBLE IN HEAVEN

THE BIBLE IN HEAVEN

This is Aqueduct speaking. Greetings, dear friend from the other side! Many of your people, when they first arrive, seem surprised that we have Bibles in heaven. Yet if the Bible is really the Word of God, as you say it is, then surely God would give His Word to us in the spirit realm, just as He does to you on earth?

Yes, we have the Holy Word, and it is the most precious thing we possess. We study it constantly. It is the source of our wisdom and inspiration, and is the principal means by which we communicate with the Lord, and by which He instructs and guides us.

In form and appearance, our Bibles differ widely. Jews generally think of God's Word as necessarily in the form of a roll, and so it is given to them in that way. (Several of your prophets saw these rolls or scrolls when their eyes were opened into heaven.) Christians have always used codexes or books with folded pages, and so God's Word in our part of heaven is usually in the form of a bound volume. I understand that in some remote regions it is inscribed on clay tablets, or written on birchbark. People like what they are accustomed to.

The language employed in all cases is the spiritual language of ideas. Just as our spoken words are shaped directly from our thoughts, so is our writing.

Each letter mirrors forth a unit of thought, and the building up of letters into words, and words into sentences, provides a full and perfect expression of our most complex ideas.

As in your earth languages, we use vowels and consonants. The consonants convey the flow of thought, while the vowels, which are written within and around the consonants, express the affections within the thought. I am told that the language on your earth which most closely resembles ours is Hebrew. Probably that is why Hebrew was originally used for the transmission of God's Word.

Anyone over here can read our language. You just fix your eyes on the letters and words written on the page, follow along the line, and the thought is fully conveyed to you. Illiterate peasants from uncivilized lands, when they wake up on this side and are given a book, find to their astonishment that they can read it. They can write also, without having to learn. Writing is natural and spontaneous over here. The hand never hesitates for a word or phrase, and the result is a perfect expression of the personality as well as the thought of the writer.

There is also a kind of projection-writing which does not have to be set down by hand. Look! I simply focus my eyes on this sheet of paper, and my thoughts appear on it, perfectly expressed in writing. You can read it easily! We cover classroom walls like this in our schools, as a teaching aid. But such projection-writing has no permanence. I turn away my head, and it disappears. To produce writing that will endure, the hand must be employed. This is because the hand is the power-tool of the body; our thoughts and affections terminate in our hands. Anyone who wants to be an author, can be. There are numerous libraries with shelves piled high with manuscript writings, all carefully classified. We also have techniques for making copies of what we write, as you have on earth.

I remarked a few moments ago that anyone in this world can read our writing. I should have qualified this by saying that the reader must have the capacity to understand the ideas conveyed. Someone once showed me some books written in one of the higher heavens, and they were meaningless to me. One of them consisted of nothing but numerals: row after row of numbers, each row beginning with a number in bold type, followed by others written smaller. I was told that every number conveyed some meaning to those who were able to receive it. The first number in each group, written large, was the subject of the thought, and those following modified and qualified the thought. These numerals, it seems, represented general concepts, and the angels who write in this way are principally interested in generalities. If anything specific is mentioned, they turn their heads away, saying, "All particulars come under general principles. We only want to know the principle which is involved."

Master copies of the Bible are written out under dictation by specially selected angels, and afterwards printed. The writer is filled by the Holy Spirit and does not know what he is writing; it is purely automatic. Copies written by different angels differ slightly in detail; this is because the Holy Spirit infills each writer only according to his capacity for reception. Thus, the resulting manuscript is precisely adapted to the needs of the writer, and those of his brethren who are similar to himself. Every community, however small, has its own specific Bible. As new communities are formed (which is continually taking place) new Bibles are dictated.

In addition to these regional variations in the text, there is a fundamental difference between the Bibles of those who particularly love the Lord, and those who particularly love the neighbor. All cover the same ground, but at different levels.

In what we might call the "Lord" Bibles, we see the Lord's life on earth lovingly dealt with in the whole Scriptures from beginning to end: the Garden of Eden, the Patriarchs, the Wanderings in the Wilderness; the Settlement in the Promised Land, the Exile, and the final return of the people to the New Jerusalem. These stories tell allegorically of the Lord's conception and birth, and of how He gradually replaced the human elements (drawn from His mother) by the divine elements (which were His own Soul); how He met all the evil spirits of hell in single combat, and repulsed them, suffering sorely in the process, yet without hate; His last temptation on the cross, and the final slip-over of consciousness from the finite to the infinite; the nature of His post-resurrection body, and the perfect union of the Humanity with Divinity when He "ascended into heaven." The theme of the whole story is Celestial Love — love of mankind by the Lord, and love of the Lord by mankind; and the variations on this theme make the most superlatively beautiful love story ever told.

In what we might call the "Neighbor" Bibles, the same area is covered, but we see the whole Scripture story, from beginning to end, as applying to human regeneration and salvation, showing how the Lord's redemptive work freed mankind, and how we can serve the Lord by serving one another. Such service to the neighbor requires a clearer understanding of truth than pure love of the Lord requires, and so these "Neighbor" Bibles are the greatest source of truth available in the universe.

Our Bibles do not contain any reference to specific places and kingdoms in your world, and the identity of the men and women referred to is veiled to such a degree that we cannot tell precisely who were the actual people involved. For instance, it would be impossible for us to locate and identify any particular patriarch, king, prophet or apostle, though all of them are alive over here somewhere.

An exception could be made, perhaps, in the case of the woman Mary, from whom our Lord derived His humanity. I have actually met her and spoken with her. Far from being "Queen of Heaven," as some of your people believe, she is a simple angel, living in one of the middle heavens. She told me she had indeed been our Lord's mother on earth, but said most emphatically that He had put off everything He had derived from her, so that she was no longer His mother, but was among the humblest of those who adore Him as God. We then spoke of other things, and the part she had contributed to His incarnation was soon forgotten between us.

If you ask me what relationship exists between our Bibles in heaven and yours on earth, I would say that ours lie within yours as a man's soul lies within his body. The Holy Word, as a projection of God's infinite mind, passes down through all the successive heavens in order, and terminates in your Bible. Thus, it is adapted at its various levels to the wisdom of the

angels in all their degrees, and also to the intelligence
of men on earth, and even of little children. Thus, the
Bible on earth helps to hold the earth and all the
heavens together like a beautiful web passing through
the structure of them all.

When you people on earth read your Bible, with
its stories of battle and adventure, its philosophy and
its poetry, we on our side draw from it just what
interests and concerns us individually, whether on the
level of love to the Lord or love to the neighbor. And,
what may seem strange, we find it even more delightful when your little children ponder its stories than
when your theologians and university professors study
them! Children have not developed the hard core of
self-love which blocks the inflow of life from heaven,
whereas most of your scholars are more or less in the
conceit of knowledge. Actually, your Bible is superior
to ours, for it contains all of ours, at all their levels,
and at the same time an external natural sense which
ours lack. In your Bible on earth, the Word of the
Lord rests in its fullness, holiness and power.

Of course it is true that your external, literal sense
acts as a covering which to a large extent hides the
power and glory of the Divine Love and Wisdom
within. This is a provision of the Divine Mercy for
communities such as yours where good and evil people
live together in close proximity. It allows for the
doubts of the agnostic and the denials of the atheist.
In our world, the Bible can be a real source of danger
to those who are evil at heart. In this Balance-Land,
all copies have to be shut carefully away in boxes or
closets, for we never know who might be around.

There was an unfortunate incident fairly recently,
when an evil spirit was on the rampage (he was here

by invitation of someone on earth, I may say!). Somehow he got into our chapel in the hospital. There was a copy of the Word open on the little altar, and he went up to it with the intention of damaging it, out of pure hatred. As he touched it, there was a violent explosion, which shook the whole building. We ran into the chapel to see what had happened, and there, as the smoke drifted away, we saw the culprit lying unconscious on the floor in a distant corner, where he had been thrown by the blast. A doctor examined him and found he was all right. We had him carried out on a stretcher and tipped over the escarpment, where he landed safely in his own place. We heard afterwards that the poor fellow was beaten up by his friends down there, because they said his clothes stank of heaven! This surprised me, because when we found him in the chapel, they definitely stank of hell!

The Word of God is very powerful. It can split mountains and pulverize rocks. It can excavate reservoirs and build cities. But for the most part we use it as a source of security, comfort and peace. It warms us when we are cold, and is a light to us in our darkness. This is literally true. In our school classes here, we start the morning in complete darkness; the teacher opens the Word, and a glimmer of light comes from it. Then, as the lessons proceed and the students begin to "see" the truth, the light from the Word grows brighter and brighter, radiating into every corner of the classroom; and when they leave at the close of the session, it is dazzling.

Each of us carries a small copy of the Word on his person. Here is mine. Is it not beautiful? See how it glows! If I rub it on my tunic, my tunic shines! Every page of it is a joy to read . . . This book is small, like a gem. I have a larger copy at home, for regular use. In our temples we have magnificent copies on the altar, beautifully written and illuminated. They are encrusted with precious stones which gleam and sparkle, and are surrounded by a glowing mist in which you can see a pulsating rainbow. Everyone sitting in the temple faces the Word. The preacher stands slightly to one side so as not to obscure it, and the light seems to flow from the Word into him, and from him to the congregation.

See, this is like a little torch! "Thy Word is a lamp unto my feet, and a light unto my path." And now, if you will excuse me, I will meditate a little on what I am reading here . . .

TWELVE

Nursery-Land

Interview 12

NURSERY-LAND

This is Aqueduct speaking. Greetings, dear friend from the other side! When babies and young children arrive here, they are handed over, with great tenderness and loving concern, to angel mothers in one of the nurseries on that mountainside over to the east. We do not see them here again. But because I had some curiosity as to what happened to them and how they were reared to maturity, the Lord once gave me permission to visit Nursery-Land.

My colleagues who have been in this reception work much longer than I have, tell of a time when a large proportion of those arriving here were infants. Thousands of little baby souls arrived every day. And the wonderful thing is that their presence in large numbers in those past ages served to counteract the evil influence of the dreadful degenerate type of adults who were coming over at that time, and so helped to maintain equilibrium in this Balance-Land. This is an example of how the Lord over-rules evil and makes it serve some use in His divine plan; fortunately conditions have improved in this New Age.

The Nursery-Land which I visited was on a kind of plateau projecting from the mountain wall, covered with grass and trees and dotted with cabins and small houses. The cliff rose almost vertically behind it, while in front the land dropped away in a series of rocky ledges. A cascade fell down the cliff, and divided in two to pass round both sides of the plateau, embracing it, as it were; it then became a single stream again, and plunged down into the valley.

I found my way first to the very center of this little paradise. The weather was warm; sheep grazed with their lambs, and doves murmured in the branches. A sweet scent of blossoms filled the air; but in this central region the flowers were perpetually in bud, whether on the trees or the bushes or on the ground. The cabins were made of golden-tinted olive wood, beautifully fashioned; rambler roses, all in bud, festooned the sides of the doorways.

A foster mother was sitting in the warm sunshine outside one of the cabins, gently rocking on a swinging seat and crooning to a tiny naked infant on her knee. I knew that the child had "died" at birth. It had been crying, but was now relaxed and content. On the grass at her feet a little lambskin rug had been spread out, and in the soft woolly fleece lay another naked baby, fast asleep. Three others, with daisy-chains around their necks, crawled in the sweet grass; one was cooing, and as he cooed a dove flew down and settled on the grass in front of him, and answered him most prettily. The mother beckoned to me, but made a sign that I was not to disturb the children. I spoke with her for awhile, but she was from a higher heaven than mine, and so communication between us was difficult.

Afterwards I left her and went towards the front of the plateau, where there was a magnificent view of the broad plain of Balance-Land, with its many schools, hospitals and reception buildings: ours was just visible in the middle distance. Here there were flocks of singing birds, and the trees and shrubs were in full blossom, for the children in this area were older — no longer in "bud." Boys and girls dressed in simple clothing were romping together. One boy was riding on a white-haired goat. They had balls which squeaked and chuckled and bounced about with a life of their own. All their toys seemed to be alive.

I approached a building which turned out to be two houses connected by a porch. On this porch or veranda sat two angels who were obviously husband and wife. (I could tell this because seen from a distance they looked like one person, and only separated out when I approached near them.) The woman was matron to six girls who lived together in one of the houses. The man was "big brother" to six boys in the other. (He was not called "father" because the Lord alone is Father to us all.) During certain periods of each day the children were allowed to play together, whereas at other times the boys were separated from the girls by a rustic fence which could be made to appear or disappear as required.

I sat with the angel couple on the front porch, and felt much more comfortable with them than with the foster mother of the babies, because they were from a lower heaven. They had some amusing stories to tell of the children, and obviously enjoyed their work. While I was there, a girl came in in tears, trying to hide a big black stain on her white dress. The matron said sternly to her: "Go inside the house and wash that spot out; the dress is ruined!" The girl went indoors, and we heard occasional sobs as she scrubbed at her dress, apparently without effect as she returned to us with the stain just as bad as ever. "Wash that dirt right out!" scolded the matron again, and again the child went inside the house and struggled to do so;

but now, if anything, the stain was worse! After the third attempt, equally futile, the matron asked, with a melting kindness, "Well, what caused it?" Then the girl broke down, and confessed to having been rude to one of her sisters who had provoked her. "Go and fetch her up here," said the matron. Soon the two girls appeared together. The other girl's dress was covered with so much dirt that she had been ashamed to let anyone see it! "Make up your quarrel," said the matron, "and be friends again." So they apologized to one another, and kissed each other; and lo! the spots vanished, and both girls' dresses became clean and neat and fresh, and they ran away together and played happily for the rest of the day.

The husband was amused, and said, "My boys are worse than the girls. Once one of them stole a lump of sugar from the kitchen closet and put it in the pocket of his pants. And when he came out of the house, smoke was coming out of his pocket! He tried to hide it, but I could hardly miss it. I asked him what mischief he had been up to, and he said, "Nothing!" At that there was a lot more smoke, and a hole burnt through, which grew bigger and bigger until the lump of sugar fell out on the ground! That really scared him, and he confessed and promised never to steal again."

The wife told me that each child had a flower garden which they cultivated assiduously, and prizes were given from time to time for the best garden. But the strange thing was that they did not cultivate the plants with their fingers so much as with their hearts and minds, because when they were good and obedient and happy together, the flowers flourished and blossomed beautifully, whereas at the slightest lapse from grace they wilted and even died. As the girls succeeded in mastering their lessons, new flowers appeared in the beds — small at first, but growing bigger as their school work progressed.

I noticed that one of the little boys looked different from the rest; he had a moustache and a scrub of a beard. When I asked about him, I was told that a few days ago he had looked like a tiny white-haired old man! In fact, he had lived in your world to a ripe old age, but had been mentally retarded all his life, and had never developed spiritually beyond the childhood state. Soon he would be just like the other children, and would grow up here and develop normally as if he had "died" in childhood. People who were mentally undeveloped from birth in your world, rapidly shrink away to infancy when they come over here, and start right at the beginning. If someone in your world has a head injury, say in adolescence, which damages the brain and impairs his freedom of choice, then no matter how old he becomes on earth, when he arrives here he reverts to the stage of development he had reached when the accident occurred. You only bring with you into this world what you have actually made your own by free decision.

Later I was taken into the classroom in the boys' house. It looked more like a playroom than a classroom, for all lessons are learned at this stage through games. The boys competed together in everything, and it was found that each one excelled in something. Their only textbook was the Word of God — with a text especially adapted to their age; and they were shown how it applied to their lives, and how they could draw upon it for help from the Lord. All the children could pray effectively, and did so regularly in their daily worship. (On your earth, too, all children can pray quite naturally, if they are not led by adults to believe that there is something phony about prayer.)

There was a special wall of the classroom on which moving pictures were shown, illustrating any subject under discussion. Most of the pictures were drawn directly from the Word of God, but I also saw a couple of parable stories illustrating moral truths. The children seemed delighted with these stories, and apparently had no difficulty in catching the hidden meaning.

I was told that on special days, for a treat, they were taken in a flying carriage to visit various regions of heaven and hell, so that they could learn about the world around them, and see human nature in all its manifestations.

The teaching here is so effective that all the children learn to overcome their hereditary evils, and develop love to the Lord and love to the neighbor, so that all eventually enter heaven. (There are no sheep lost from this fold!) But before taking up their permanent life as angels in heaven, they are placed back in Balance-Land, and have to find their own way to heaven like everybody else, and enter by one of the ordinary routes. They are not given any preferential treatment! However, these "Children of the Household" can usually be recognized because of a certain shyness and sensitivity, a tenderness and delicacy of temperament, which unfits them for many kinds of employment, though qualifying them admirably for others.

I was told how they find their marriage partners when they reach Balance-Land. (Every complete angel is a married pair; I am single only because, unfortunately for me, my beloved wife has not yet joined me.) There is a kind of predestination with those who grow up in this world. Such predestination does not operate on your earth, for there everybody has freedom of choice, and every time this freedom is exercised the character changes slightly; so it is impossible to tell who a person's future partner will be (except by divine foresight!). But with those who die in childhood and grow up on this side, there is no real free will; they have to act in accordance with their ruling love, as it has been developed by their teachers on the basis of the natures which they inherited from their parents.

The foster mother and teachers know from the beginning that such-and-such a boy will be the soul mate of such-and-such a girl, and have been secretly preparing them for eventual union. Nothing is revealed, however, until they are in Balance-Land. Then, as if by chance, they meet somewhere, perhaps in a crowd. The young man sees the girl, and his heart jumps and races, and he knows instantly, "She is the one I have been dreaming of!" He approaches her shyly and gets into conversation, and she says in her heart, "I am his and he is mine!" Very soon they reveal their feelings and become betrothed, and travel together through the final stages until they reach the frontier of heaven; and then, oh bliss! they accept each other as husband and wife before the Lord, and are united and enter heaven as one.

Life for these youngsters is very sweet, but it is far from ideal. They never acquire the sturdiness of those who are allowed their full time in the rough-and-tumble of the earth school. As conditions in your world improve with the dawning of this New Age, there will be fewer cases of premature death, and gradually the number of occupants of these Nursery-Lands will decrease. It is never the Lord's will that anyone should die in childhood; it is always better for the fruit to remain on the tree and ripen on your side before it is plucked. There are so many different types of mature adults coming over from your earth, that all the necessary functions in the heavenly economy could be catered for without parents over there having to suffer the agonizing loss of babies and children. Nursery-Land is the Lord's way of coping with a disorderly condition, which He must permit in the present circumstances. But as always, He makes the very best of a bad job.

After I had said good-bye to my new friends, and was walking towards the edge of the plateau, I saw a little boy standing and gazing wistfully out over the sunlit plain. I greeted him and asked him what he was thinking about. He said he had had a wonderful dream, in which he had seen a kind and beautiful lady, far away, who knew about him, and was thinking of him, and praying for him. I asked him if this was his mother, and he said, "Oh no, my mother is here in the house; I have never seen this dream lady. But oh, I love her dearly, and I know she will come here one day, and I shall take her hand and we shall go together into our Father's presence." I said to him, "Perhaps, when this lady comes, she will have her husband with her?" The child's face shone. "Yes," he said, "he was also in my dream. The three of us will go together!"

Good-bye, and God bless you.

THIRTEEN

GLOSSALALIA

GLOSSALALIA

*This is Aqueduct speaking. Greetings, dear friend
from the other side!* Do you see that old woman over
there? She has just arrived from your world. Watch
her. She stretches her arms high up above her head
with the palms facing upwards. Her wrinkled face is
suffused with joy and simple submission, as she cries:
"Hallelujah, Praise the Lord, Amen." How different
people are, one from another! We in our community
have never been outwardly demonstrative, and I
personally should find it difficult and unnatural to
raise my arms like that. Yet with her, in her innocence,
it is touchingly expressive.

This woman is from a group who claim to have been
baptized with the Holy Spirit and to speak with
tongues. Perhaps you have seen something of this
"Glossalalia" movement? It is interesting and signifi-
cant, though not so important perhaps as those who
belong to it believe.

I have been told, by Guardians who have investi-
gated the subject, that there are two kinds of speaking
with tongues. The first is by far the most common. It
involves a bypassing of the rational mind, including
the memory-system where the sound-symbols of your
language are housed. The thoughts and feelings of the
heart well up through secret channels and bring pres-

sure to bear on the vocal cords, which vibrate as if of their own accord.

Those who practice speaking with tongues as a religious rite, often claim that it is the Holy Spirit speaking through them; but this is only true to the extent that their own inner thoughts and feelings are derived from the Holy Spirit — which, of course, is the outpouring power of God.

What they are actually doing is analogous to what we do when we speak in the spiritual language. They clothe their thoughts with sound. The irony is that we in the spiritual world cannot hear them, because their speech vibrations are in the physical atmosphere; and nobody in the physical world can understand them, because nobody has the genuine faculty of spiritual interpretation (though some claim to have). These people call themselves Pentecostalists, from the incident which took place in Jerusalem at the Pentecost Feast after our Lord's Ascension. But there the crowds had their inner senses quickened into the spiritual world, so that they could communicate in the spiritual language, which everybody conscious in the spiritual world understands.

When these glossalalia initiates come over here at death, it seems to them that they are still speaking with tongues, but now it is the common means of expression. Everybody here is speaking with tongues! This discovery gives great delight to those who are good at heart; they are overjoyed to find others sharing a grace-gift which has been so precious to themselves. Others who are evil become jealous and indignant.

Since glossalalia in your world cannot be understood and does not communicate anything rationally, what is the use of it? I have often asked that question, and have been told by those who have worked with Pentecostalists that it does serve a use. It is, in fact, a wonderful antidote for an over-dependence on the rational faculty such as is characteristic of your western culture. It can be therapeutic, in that it encourages the speaker to relax and submit himself to the operation of forces from within. With tightly bound-up souls, it produces a sense of release from tension, a liberation, an increase of vigor, an upsurge of joy.

(Watch that woman over there! She is bubbling over with tenderness and happiness and spiritual vitality. Truly the Holy Spirit is working in her!)

The ability to speak with tongues is, however, no evidence that the speaker is either good or evil. *"By their fruits ye shall know them."* If an esoteric practice leads, in your world, to a deepening of love to the Lord and to one's fellows, then it is good; but if it leads your people to feel superior and to look down with contempt on others who are perhaps developing along different lines, then it is evil. Remember, the spiritual language is spoken in hell as well as in heaven!

So far I have been referring to only one kind of glossalalia, where thoughts are expressed directly in sound. But there is another kind, in which the speaker *does* use an earthly language, which is identifiable, and can be readily understood by anyone versed in that language, though it may be totally unknown to the speaker himself. More surprising still, he may be using an archaic form of some earth language, or a language which has not been spoken for generations.

This is analogous to what is called "long memory." Do you know what that is? A person is said to have "long memory" when he claims to remember events which took place a long time before he was born. Evidence that certain people on earth possess such memory has led some of your scholars to a belief in Reincarnation — the theory that spirits re-enter your earth life from over here by rebirth, over and over again, and that the memory of former incarnations can persist. My friend, this theory is purely imaginary; it has no basis in fact. Personally I cannot understand why anyone should think that the Lord would demote them and make them go through the same grades of the school course over and over again. Progress, in fact, is always upwards, never downwards.

The true explanation of "long memory" is to be found in quite another direction. It derives from the fact which was made clear to you early in our meetings together, that every man, woman and child on earth is associated all the time with spirits, good and evil. Often these spirits enter into a man's thoughts, and they can be deceived into thinking that his thoughts are their own. On rare occasions (and this is quite disorderly) the reverse takes place. The man enters into the thoughts of one of his attendant spirits, and believes that the spirit's thoughts are his own.

Now it is a fact that all spirits, whether angels or devils, carry with them the memory of everything they learnt and everything they did or that happened to them in their former existence on earth. Normally we are unable to recall these things, because the natural degree of our mind is closed. We cannot speak any of the languages of your earth, or visualize the situations in which we were involved there. Most of us are even unaware that our earthly memory is still with us, since it belongs to a phase of life we have since outgrown. It is like a little closed box somewhere at the back of our minds. Only when the Lord wants to remind us of something we thought or did, or determined to do, or not to do, in the earth life, does He remove the lid and let us see. Then we are usually horrified at the vision of what we were, and thank Him from our hearts for the progress we have made.

Now, if we are associated with people in your world who are striving desperately hard to get through to our thoughts, it is quite likely that they will tap the natural degree of our minds which was built up when we were in their present stage of development. Thoughts and images from our memory will leak through into theirs, and they will seem to themselves to be recalling things which in fact happened to *us*, not to them at all — some incident or event which took place centuries ago according to earthly reckoning. This happens most commonly in dreams, but it can do also in the waking state. Moreover, our old language mechanism is available to them, though not to us; they can enter into it and use it as if it were their own. This explains how people on earth can speak correctly in a language they have never even heard of, or perhaps a language that has not been in use for hundreds of years.

Your clever historians who are trying to reconstruct the whole story of mankind might avail themselves of this source of information concerning doubtful events of the long-distant past. All the characters are here in the spirit world, very much alive; and all the facts of their earthly existence, together with a full explanation of their motivation, are minutely recorded in their natural memories. They themselves cannot recall them; but perhaps you earth-folk, working from your side, might ferret things out. Why not commission those among you with the faculty of "long memory" to develop their potentials and extend their range — and encourage others to cultivate the technique?

However, I hope this will *not* come about, as it would be an embarrassment to us on this side if we were continually in demand to provide information concerning our doings in the former life, of which in many cases we are deeply ashamed.

How strange that anyone should want to record past events! The past is the one thing that everyone has left behind, and therefore is of no further importance. Our only interest here is in the *present* — how we can best serve our beloved Lord and our fellow beings; and in the *future* — how we can improve our relations with Him and with one another.

Already I am beginning to feel my thoughts have been away from Him for too long. I must get back into a consciousness of His presence.

See that woman over there? She is throwing up her hands again in joyous, spontaneous worship. I will bid you good-bye and go and join her . . . Excuse me if I raise my arms a little, as she is doing, with the palms upwards, *so* . . . something impels me to it. *Hallelujah, hallelujah! Praise the Lord! Amen!*

FOURTEEN

THE NEEDLE'S EYE

THE NEEDLE'S EYE

This is Aqueduct speaking. Greetings, dear friend from the other side! Seeing you again reminds me of how I made a fool of myself at our last interview, raising my hands, palms upward, and shouting *Hallelujah* like a Pentecostalist! I have been chuckling over it ever since, and I love that old woman for having been the cause of humbling my silly pride. She is already in a very high heaven.

* * * * * *

I have just been conversing with an extremely proud man. He claims to have been the richest man in the world. That may be only his image of himself, but I have no doubt he was a multi-millionaire. He made his money, he said, from selling oil — for some purpose which I do not understand. He did not manufacture the oil. It was given to the world by God as a free gift for everyone, so why this one man was allowed to profit from it to that extent I cannot imagine. But then, so many things about your world are puzzling to us over here, though we may have understood them once upon a time.

Another surprising thing is that this man should actually boast about his wealth, although the church throughout the ages has condemned riches. Our Lord, Himself, said, "It is easier for a camel to go through the eye of a needle than for a rich man to enter into the kingdom of God.'' You would think our friend would be ashamed of it and try to hide the fact of his wealth now he is over here; but there he goes, proclaiming it to anyone who will listen to him!

Obviously, worldly wealth is neither good nor evil in itself. But those who set their heart on riches generally allow their inner spiritual faculties to wither and die through lack of exercise, so that when they enter this world they are like our friend there, who is practically a half-wit. It is amazing to think that in your world he was probably regarded as a man of outstanding intelligence and acumen; a director of companies, perhaps a pillar of some church somewhere; but here he just mooches around with no interest in anything. He is so sick in mind that we shall have to wait until he has recovered somewhat, and adjusted himself to the new environment, before we know whether we can get him to heaven, or whether he will just drift away and join the aimless population in one of the regions of hell.

Rich people, when they discover they are bereft of everything they valued, often behave in quite fantastic ways. They loudly lament what they regard as a financial crash. One ex-millionaire, realizing his loss, tried to commit suicide; and only when he found that the knife passed right through his throat without hurting him, did he fully accept the fact that he was ''dead'' already, and had nowhere else to escape to!

Not all cases are quite so dramatic. A wealthy man who came over recently was so distressed over the loss of his money, that I took pity on him and asked him if he would like us to set him up with a million dollars. At first he was incredulous, then overwhelmed

with joy, though he modestly suggested that a hundred
thousand would do to begin with. We made him a nice
little strong-room with metal door and a secret lock
which only he could open, and we piled the shelves
with bundles of twenty dollar bills. (It was all fantasy, of course, but everyone who saw them said the
bills were very realistic.) How that man gloated over
his hoard! For a while he spent all his time in that
dimly-lit closet, counting out the bills and arranging
them with the heads the same way up. But when he
came out with his pockets bulging, he was amazed to
find that he could not interest anyone in them. Shops?
Yes, there are shops around here, of course; but anyone can take what he needs, without money and without
price; so what particular advantage did these dollars
give him? He surreptitiously offered a bundle of bills
as a gift to one of the angel guards, who laughed mer-
rily and accepted it, as if he were playing a game with
a little boy; our friend perceived this, and was ashamed
and confused. Then, after a few days, he was horrified
to discover that his strong-room was overrun by mice,
who were chewing up the dollar bills to make a nest.
He tried desperately to clear them out, but they kept
coming back.

Eventually he approached me for help. As we talked
together, he began to realize what a fool he had been,
and to understand that money is valueless in this
world, since everything we need is given to us as a
free gift from our heavenly Father, nor is it possible
for anyone to have an advantage over others by virtue
of the possession of some little pieces of paper. As
soon as he had relinquished his emotional hold on
that hoard of money, the whole lot disappeared, strong-
room, mice and all. And, in fact, he was relieved at

heart to be rid of the encumbrance, and felt free now to develop his inner nature which he had neglected for so long. He has since quite recovered, praise the Lord, and has gone on into heaven through the needle's eye — but, not as a rich man!

The wealthy in your world have peculiar difficulties and temptations, which more than outweigh the advantages of the luxury in which they live. I am truly thankful that I grew up in a poor family, where we thought of ourselves as nobodies. A rich man is bound to take himself seriously and consider himself important, since everyone tells him he is (usually in the hope of getting something out of him). Living as he does in comfortable surroundings, with servants and employees to do his slightest bidding, how can he avoid the corrosive effect of complacence and self-satisfaction? And the fact that he wields so much power on the physical and social level leads him to think he is master of his fate and the captain of his soul, and this blinds him to the operation of the Lord's Providence. Looking out on his own works, he declares, like King Nebuchadnezzar of old, ''Is not this great Babylon that I have built, by the might of my power and for the honor of my majesty?'' Then, having built his empire, he must maintain it, and this requires constant vigilance. He lives in a state of fear lest he should make a false move or something should happen to cause disaster. He has established a standard of living which is inexorable. His possessions become like a monster which he must feed with an increasing quantity of food, and if he fails to do so for one day, the monster will turn and rend him. He becomes a slave to his own wealth. Truly, it is hard for a rich

man to enter into the kingdom of heaven; his camel-
loads of possessions keep him outside.

Some manage it, however. Not all rich men are
ruined by their wealth, or become enslaved by it. Some
succeed in developing a spiritual nature within and
behind their wordly activities. If a businessman wants
to know whether he is on the road to heaven, let him
ask himself honestly: "Am I doing what I do to help
my fellowman, or merely to amass wealth and power
and prestige for myself?" If a man's motivation is
the love of use, of being useful to society, then he will
continue to exercise his faculties here in the spiritual
world, for heaven is a kingdom of uses. Some of the
angels who are in the highest executive positions,
organizing the welfare of large numbers of their fellow angels according to the Lord's divine plan, were
once successful businessmen on earth.

During past ages, when the verdict of the Church had
more influence than it does today, many people, scared
by the Church's condemnation of wealth, gave themselves up to the solitary life of pious meditation. Some
of these solitaries developed such a profound love for
the Lord that they are now far away in the highest
celestial heaven. They are utterly beyond my range
of thought; I cannot even see them, let alone understand what they are doing, though I know they are
helping to mediate God's love to the whole of creation.
But, on the other hand, some who gave themselves up
to solitude and self-mortification, did so merely because they were interested in their own salvation.
These despised others in comparison with themselves,
and developed a harsh and gloomy disposition, so
that when they arrived over here they were scandal-

ized by the free, joyous life of heaven, and turned away in disgust, preferring to seek out some desert place where they could continue to live as they did in the world, thanking God they were not as other men. They are still there.

The love of power is much the same as the love of wealth. If a man seeks power in order to help other people and bring about improvements in society, then he develops a heavenly disposition, and is given a position of power in heaven. "Well done, good and faithful servant," says our Lord, "you have been faithful over a few things, I will make you ruler over many." Some of our greatest rulers were once kings and famous statesmen on earth. Not all were, of course. Some who had great potentials of leadership were so poor and lowly on earth that they had no opportunities of developing them; over here they quickly came to the fore. On the other hand, self-seeking tyrants, whether political, social or domestic, and whether from the governing or laboring classes (for there are tyrants and bullies in every stratum of society on earth): these soon find their way to hell, where they quarrel and fight one another mercilessly as each tries to dominate the rest.

I sense, my friend, that you are surprised to hear me refer to "rulers" in heaven. But in any well-ordered society there must be people in authority, of higher and lower rank. In heaven we have princes and governors in all kinds of administrative positions; also judges and arbitrators and lawyers to settle and explain difficult cases (our law being God's Law); teachers, preachers, doctors (you would call them psychiatrists), and so on. All look to the Lord for guidance in their various functions and do their work for Him, and everything works smoothly, being lubricated by love.

I wish I could take you to visit the Prince who administers the region where I live. (We call him "Prince" not "King," since the Lord is our only King.) He would be pleased to welcome you. However, you do not appear to be very mobile yet in our world. Admittedly you are no longer like a ghost or apparition, as you were when we first began this little experiment of communication. Yet you still have that disconcerting trick of vanishing when I turn my thoughts away from you! And I always see you in the same spot, under this tree. Well, since you cannot accompany me in person, I will describe a visit I made recently to the palace, to present a group of new arrivals to our Prince.

*   *   *   *   *   *

They were already accustomed to the brilliant white light and genial warmth of our atmosphere, and were quite at ease as I led them up a steep path through the woods over there to our metropolis, which crowns the hilltop. We were admitted through three successive gates, and so entered the main street. Few people were about, because it was morning and the inhabitants were in their homes or places of occupation; even the windows were shut. So, to occupy the time till noon, I showed my friends around the city. We saw avenues and public squares with flowerbeds and fountains, and streams running along the roadside under graceful bridges. It is difficult to describe the style of architecture of the mansions and palaces, especially as certain features are always changing, as in a kaleidoscope. The general effect is of enormous semi-transparent stones glistening and sparkling in the light of the sun. The prince's palace is at the very summit of the hill, in the central square of the city. It is built of porphyry on a substructure of jasper. At the entrance are six lofty blue columns made of lapis lazuli. The roof is of small overlapping gold plates, which catch and reflect the light, and the tall crystal windows are framed with gold. But what does all this mean to one who has not seen for himself the living quality of every object in heaven?

We entered the vestibule of the palace, and I introduced my companions to one of the guards, who conducted us through some of the rooms, pointing out ornaments of amazing beauty: silver tables inlaid with gold, and articles upon them made of entire gems beautifully carved. The walls and ceilings were embellished with intricate designs, which led the eye ever inward and upward. My companions were so struck by the wonder of what they saw that I had to check them, reminding them that these objects are the handiwork of the Lord Himself, and their value lies not in what they are, but in the way they lead us to meditate on the ineffable beauty of His Love and Wisdom.

Eventually, a messenger came to say we were to lunch with the Prince. My companions were taken aside and given suitable garments: a brown toga and a tunic of iridescent silk. (You see, I myself am wearing the same kind of outfit.) Before they could put these on, my friends had to effect a temporary change in their state, bringing themselves for the time being into harmony with the particular quality of thought which characterizes our region, and to which the clothes correspond.

Soon there was a chiming of bells, and we went out into the courtyard. The upper windows were now open, and we could hear singing coming from within. We hurried to a portico, where a number of important officials were waiting. The great carved doors swung open, and a formal procession came through. The Prince was in the middle; before him were his advisers and counsellors, and after him the chief men of the court, followed by guards. I humbly presented my companions to the Prince as he passed by. He smiled and bowed graciously, and, without stopping, bade us all welcome and invited us to follow with the others into the dining hall.

We were each given our places at an enormous table magnificently spread. In the center was a huge pyramid of embossed gold-work, with little projecting shelves on which were about a hundred small dishes in triple order, containing cakes, cookies and fruit. From the top of the pyramid, a fountain of delicious-smelling wine rose high into the air, and fell down in little jets into a circle of cups around the base, each cup being cut from a single pellucid gem. All over the table were silver dishes loaded with choice food of every imaginable variety.

Our Prince is a handsome and commanding man, very youthful in appearance. He was dressed on this occasion in a long purple robe embroidered with silver stars; under it was a violet tunic of shining silk. On his breast hung a gold medallion surrounded by diamonds. These garments imaged forth his keen and profound intelligence. He is the wisest of us all, yet one of the humblest, kindest and simplest men that ever lived.

* * * * * *

But ah, I see I am wearying you. This interview has already been too long, and is proving too great a strain on both of us. I must tell you the rest some other time. However, I have said enough to indicate that, at least in some regions of heaven, there is a very high level of wealth and magnificence. On the other hand, nobody here owns anything personally, so nobody is rich. All of us are equally poor in the sight of the Lord, and in our own eyes. We possess nothing, we merit nothing, we are nothing. Only because of our own personal emptiness can we receive such unlimited bounty from our Father and King.

"Blessed are the poor. Blessed are the meek. Blessed are they who hunger and thirst after righteousness, for they shall be filled." May you learn to receive these blessings, even while you are still in the natural world — as you certainly can do. May you learn to think nothing of wealth and power, valuing only the riches of our Father's love.

Good-bye, and God bless you.

FIFTEEN

The Hospital

THE HOSPITAL

This is Aqueduct speaking. Greetings, dear friend from the other side! I have been working all day in our hospital, and shall be glad to have a chat with you before I fly back home. Not that I am a doctor, of course; but some of our new arrivals have been admitted for treatment, so I, as their Receptionist, have been in attendance.

People seem surprised that there should be sickness and hospitals in the spirit world, yet I do not know why they should be surprised, considering how much is being said in your world about psychosomatic diseases.

One patient in particular, who arrived here yesterday, is in a very sick condition. She is sick for no other reason than that she *wants* to be sick; and, in this spiritual environment, we all get just what we want — whether we *like* it or not! Her story is a sad one. She had married an affluent husband, and lived in comfort and self-indulgence, and when he died she felt she had lost everything. Not that she had ever loved him, or he her; but by being his wife she had enjoyed status which she now felt she had lost. To bolster her self-esteem, she gave generous presents to her friends, which embarrassed and alienated them. Then, in her loneliness, she became introspective, imagining all sorts of symptoms of sickness, which she hoped might make people sorry for her. Unfortunately, as she thought about these symptoms, they actually began to appear in her body; she really was ill. She went to her doctor for examination, and derived satisfaction from the thought that she was important to him, at least while he was examining her. Discussing symptoms with him increased the sense of self-importance, and the intimacy of them eased her loneliness. The doctor realized her need, and examined her frequently, knowing that this was all she really wanted. And so she continued, getting worse and worse, with full encouragement from her physician, until she died. As she woke up here after resuscitation, she was seized with agonies of pain, and began to suffer all the frightful diseases she had envisaged for herself while in the flesh.

Beware of how you use your imagination! It can create, or destroy!

Fortunately, such cases are fairly easy to treat. As she finds she can get attention and be loved and respected for what she *is,* she will drop her insane desire for sickness, and her health will be restored. The cure could easily have been effected on earth, if she had only realized that she could get all the love she needed, by involving herself unconditionally with other people, or losing herself in some useful concern outside herself and larger than herself. This might have been easier if her husband had left her penniless and she had been forced to work for her living, for work is a great healer.

Above all, she might have received healing through prayer, for she was a praying person, and was frequently on her knees. But her prayers were always self-centered, even when she was confessing her sins. They were merely an extension of her self-pity, and so achieved no contact with the Lord. If only she had been able to open up a two-way channel of communication with her heavenly Father by prayer, what a difference that would have made! All her loneliness would have disappeared, for she would have obtained a wonderful inner companionship with Him. Finding herself important in His eyes (as we all are), she would have been content to be what she actually *was,* and not put on an act and pretend to be something different, and not nearly so attractive! And with this growing contentment, her sicknesses would have been healed.

More difficult is it to cure those poor people whose psychosomatic diseases are due to resentments which have gone down so deep that they, themselves, are unaware that they have them. Memory is a wonderful thing. What you feed into it is stored there forever; it is your Book of Life. And elements in your memory, even though you may no longer be conscious of them, affect your body — both your physical body and your spiritual body. Hidden resentments which were never resolved manifest themselves as cancerous growths, digestive upsets, headaches, paralysis, all kinds of troubles. And, of course, the symptoms increase tremendously *after the death of the physical body,* when the patient arrives here; for the physical body has a pattern of health stamped upon it, and tends to resist the negative action of the mind, whereas the spiritual body responds completely.

It is largely with hidden resentments that our doctors concern themselves in this hospital. They bring the festering memory to the surface so that the patient can see it, and then they help him dispose of it, if he wishes to do so. Only when a man is stripped bare and knows himself for what he really is, can he choose to go to heaven or hell: and that choice is, of course, the Judgment. If the disease does not yield to treatment, the probability is that it has penetrated through into the ruling love, in which case the patient will almost certainly choose hell.

All the occupants of hell are in a diseased condition, though mercifully many of them do not recognize this fact. I have seen with my own eyes the frightful deformities, the scabs and yawning sores. People with leprosy, people like living corpses, people with the back of the head fallen in like a broken egg-shell. Spiritual sickness arises from the choice of evil rather than good: an inversion of loves, putting love of self in the first place, love of other people second, and love of the Lord last. True health, as we find it everywhere in heaven, results from placing love of the Lord first, love of the neighbor second, and love of self last.

There is another kind of psychological disease which we call "conscience sickness." What is conscience? It is the voice of God (usually heard through guardian angels) reminding you of what you have in the past accepted as your ideal of conduct. If you act below that ideal, conscience says: *"You know you don't want to do that! It's unworthy of you! You are acting now from your lower self, not your higher. Stop it!"* Two different people's consciences may tell them to do opposite things, because they may have accepted different ideals of conduct. Conscience can only say:

"Live according to what you believe to be right!" If you stifle conscience and act against its admonitions, it will go underground. But it will still struggle desperately to be heard, and its muffled protests will reach you in the form of stomach ulcers, headaches, and so on — even cancer. The cure? Bring conscience out of its prison, un-gag it, and restore it to its proper place of authority over your actions. Feed it regularly with truths from God's Holy Word, and obey it implicitly, and the symptoms will disappear.

The good thing about conscience sickness is that the conscience must be *still alive,* though gagged. The worse the symptoms, the more vigorous the conscience is found to be, and the greater the likelihood of complete recovery. The danger is when the symptoms begin to subside without treatment; this almost certainly indicates that the conscience is dying or dead. Once the conscience is dead, there is no hope for the patient. That is the condition of hell.

Many of the sicknesses and diseases of your earthly life are due to these same psychological disturbances, but obviously some are not. There are epidemic diseases which everybody catches, whether they are mentally disturbed or not. You can suffer from lack of certain food vitamins, or break a limb in an automobile accident. In such cases, when the patient wakes up over here after the death of the physical body, he is perfectly whole and healthy. (On the other hand, I remember a case where a man who had had only one leg during most of his life on earth, woke up here still with only one leg, because that was all he expected himself to have! I had to reason with him for quite a while before he would relinquish his hallucination and joyously allow the missing leg to reappear!)

So, you see, there are three areas of disease: physical, psychological, and spiritual. The first kind is in the physical body only, and is left behind in the grave at death. (Death is, in fact, its ultimate cure!) The second is in the mind only (the *psyche*), and can be cured in this Balance-Land after death. The third is of the spirit, the inner love: and, as far as we know, it is fatal.

The Lord never deserts any one of His children. He resides, in all the fulness of His divinity, in the inmost soul of every one of us, in saint and sinner alike, in the highest angel and the lowest devil. He is intimately present within each one of us, working ceaselessly for our salvation. If only each one of us could realize this, and draw on the infinite resources of health available within our own souls, all sickness and inadequacy and evil would vanish, like mist in the morning sunshine; and we should appear as we really are: princes and princesses, every one of us! Glorious children of light!

Will the evil spirits of hell ever enter into their true heritage? Or will they remain in their present dreadful state to eternity? I have often asked my heavenly Father that burning question, ever since I was permitted to journey to those direful regions and observe the inhabitants with my own eyes. Would they never receive healing?

To this my Lord has always replied: *"Beloved, each one of these is a beloved child of mine, even as you yourself are. Health and wholeness are freely available for them all. I am holding blessings out for them to take. If any child of mine in hell would accept one single little blessing, and take one step upwards out of that land of darkness into the light, then all the angels of heaven would rejoice and clap their hands! And my divine hunger and thirst would be to that extent relieved."*

Whither shall I go, Lord, from Your Spirit? If I ascend up into heaven, You are there. If I make my bed in hell, behold, You are there! If I say, surely the darkness shall cover me: even the night shall be light about me . . .

(Here the Angel Aqueduct became lost in meditation, and the interview was ended.)

SIXTEEN

MUSIC AND THE ARTS

MUSIC AND THE ARTS

This is Aqueduct speaking. Greetings, dear friend from the other side! Can you hear music? A composer has just arrived from your world, and ever since he has been with us the air has been full of exquisite harmony. There he is, seated on the grass under that flowering shrub, hands clasped around his knees, face looking upwards, eyes closed. Listen! He is thinking musically, and as he does so, wafts of melody float around him and upward to the Lord.

As you can hear, he is a creative musician. Not all musicians are creative. The majority are interpreters only; they do not make music of their own, but attach themselves to some composer, and receive from him. His music vibrates around him, seemingly coming from his head or heart, and most of it goes inward or upward, and can only be heard by those who are in tune with him. The interpreters receive music from him, and resonate it (often deepening and improving it by adding some insight of their own), and then direct it outward to other people, who now hear it fully.

My composer friend tells me that even during his earth-life his brain was always teeming with melodies and rhythms and progressions of chords. A modulation would form itself in his mind, and he would listen to it critically. "That's a cliche!" he would protest, and try to wash it out, as if it were something dirty. Or, "That's too sweet!" and he would flatten or sharpen one of the constituent notes to make it more sour, then pucker his lips with pleasure at the astringent taste. His wife would ask him what he was thinking about. He would shrug his shoulders and say, *"Just music!"* For hours at a time he would think entirely in music. He would repeat a musical passage over and over again, compressing it, stretching it, squashing it flat, deliberately twisting it out of shape, testing it in a hundred different forms. He would think up a phrase, and then strip all the musical verbiage from it, leaving it stark and bare like a skeleton. Or, he would fashion another phrase with all the graceful embellishments he could devise, then laugh at it for being so *rococo,* and sweep it out of his mind.

In your world, this wealth of improvised music was lost, because it was soundless; nobody was aware of it except himself. But here in the spirit world, it all pours out of him, and anyone who is in sympathy can hear and enjoy it.

Will this composer become an angel, you ask? Yes, actually he will. But whether a musician goes to heaven or hell, has nothing to do with his musicianship. It depends solely upon his relations with God and his fellowmen. It is true that this man was not "religious," in the accepted sense. He did not attend church. It was customary for his set to denounce religion as hypocrisy, and to regard all preachers as obnoxious. But in his heart he glorified his Maker with his music. He was kindly and liberal minded, and thought little of himself; and so he is already looking eagerly toward heaven. When he leaves here to begin his journey eastward, his music will become more and more God-centered, until it is nothing but heavenly harmony.

Unfortunately, some musicians who have passed through my hands are now in hell. They are still creating music — yes, music of the most strident and disturbing quality. It is quite frightening! They are followed by gangs of disciples who increase the cacophony, and acclaim themselves as pioneers of new art forms, which are in fact as old as hell itself.

Much the same can be said of the artists or painters who come over from your world. We had some recently from a "free-love" set, who explained that moral standards were different among artists from what they were with ordinary mortals. In order to be creative, they said, artists had to rebel against the conventions of society, and give complete freedom to their self-expression. When they first arrived here, they expected to be damned for their loose behavior, and were perhaps a trifle disappointed when we made nothing of it. We are not judges; we condemn nobody. Evil condemns itself.

So they started a free-love group here in Balance-Land, in which artistic expression could flourish untrammelled, in an atmosphere of sex. No one hindered them; they could do what they pleased. But, as their externals began to drop away, those who were good at heart grew sick of their own loose morals, and started looking for something more satisfying. However, habits are not easy to break. They strove for purity, but the memory of old love-entanglements kept recurring. One man confessed to me that he was being haunted by ghosts of former mistresses, each of whom claimed some part of him, so that he felt he was being wrenched and torn asunder. What agonies that poor man suffered, and how he wished he had lived more continently on earth!

In the end, all who are good at heart outlive their promiscuity, and each chooses one of the opposite sex, and they become united together as husband and wife, and live chastely in heaven. The two, as a team, produce far more beautiful works of art than they had ever achieved previously. Their art flows out of them, and surrounds them with gracious forms and glorious colors.

To visit an artists' colony in heaven is a memorable experience, and I thank the Lord that He has allowed me to do so on more than one occasion. Everything is so much more vivid there than elsewhere. One's visual faculties are keener. Instead of seeing a row of trees as just a row of trees, you perceive their branches as beautiful shapes interacting one with another. The *form* of every object becomes all-important, and, as you concentrate your attention on it, all inessentials drop away, and you find yourself face to face with the pure beauty in its quintessence. Was I ever an artist? No, no! But if you are among artists in this spirit world, their sphere enters into you and affects you, and makes you think and feel as they do.

Poets are less easily identified than musicians or artists, for the poet uses the same medium of expression as everyone else — language. The peculiarity of the poet lies not in his capacity to express himself (for everyone here can do that perfectly), but in the intensity of his thoughts and feelings. Many people become

poets over here who had no particular literary training on earth. Their feelings are extraordinarily sensitive, so that they have only to fix their thoughts on
any object of beauty or any pregnant truth, and poetry
pours out. On the other hand, some who were regarded
as great poets on earth, here become banal and trite.
Maybe they gained their reputation by mystifying
their readers with strange words and phrases; but over
here all pretense is laid aside. They have to say exactly
what they mean, which is often scarcely worth saying!

A genuine poet once told me about his inspiration.
It seems that on certain occasions, while in your world,
he had a strong desire to compose a poem on a certain
theme, but nothing would come forth. He struggled
and labored in vain. Then, some time later (next day
perhaps), he felt a kind of stirring within. He seized
writing materials, and the complete poem poured out,
almost as fast as he could set it down. The ancients
believed that in such cases a discarnate spirit or
genius was dictating the poem, so the poet who worked
in this way was said to have a *"genius."* And there is
truth in this explanation. What actually happens is
that certain spirits on this side are attracted to the
poet during his struggle for expression, and try to
help him; but, owing to the very intensity of the
struggle, he cannot receive anything from them. Later,
when he is relaxed, and especially when he has newly
awakened from sleep, the spirits distill off the flavor
of his thoughts and give it to him, adding something
of their own. Of course, all this is done in the language
of ideas (such as we are using now.) His capacity to
write down lines and verses in his language depends
to a large extent upon his mental gifts and previous

training. The *thoughts* are there, and the *drive* is there; the actual words come easily enough. Such poets are at a great advantage when they "die" and come over here, for they can now see their attendant spirits and collaborate consciously with them. A lovely give-and-take is achieved, and the results are sometimes so exquisite that the poet himself is lost in wonder.

And the other arts? Yes, surely, there are architects in heaven, and the buildings they produce are beautifully proportioned, gracious and welcoming. My own home is seemingly part of myself; it actually feels like a living thing around me. Landscape gardening, too, has been carried to perfection. The gardens are like parks in which everything shines: the leaves glisten as if made of silver, the fruit glows like gold, and the flowers in their beds form rainbows.

One interesting feature of our landscape gardening is the use of animals and birds for decorative purposes. This has been done on earth, I believe, with deer and peacocks and such-like, but not to the extent that it is practiced here. The main difference between your animals and ours is that yours have their own life cycle from generation to generation, and propagate and live independent of man; but our animals here are produced by the affections of the people who live in the neighborhood. Usually we are quite unaware of the fact that we are producing and sustaining the animals and birds which correspond to our affections; we just see them around us, and take them for granted. It is possible, however, to bring new creatures into existence by an effort of will — although these usually vanish again when the effort is relaxed.

People who loved pets when they were in your world,

like to have similar pets here, at any rate during their
first state after death. One lady remembered a particular dog which she had loved in the earth life, and
actually managed to produce it out of her own mind,
and there it was, wagging its tail, and behaving exactly
as she wanted it to. She scratched it behind the ears,
and talked to it like a baby: *"Who said little wuff-wuff
didn't have a soul?"*

Yes, we have dog shows and cat shows and horse
shows here in Balance-Land — even pig shows, if you
will believe it. And since these are a form of self-
expression on the part of the producers of the beasts,
I include them in my account of the arts. But we do
not get such vulgarity actually in heaven: just a few
beautiful creatures to add a finishing touch to our
gardens.

All our senses are catered for. Naturally we have
color symphonies. I have sat for a whole afternoon
watching the colors increase and diminish and change
and blend, and have been in turn excited and calmed
thereby. And we have perfume symphonies, of which
you on earth know nothing, since your sense of smell
has become atrophied. (Only your dogs understand
about it!) A perfume artist controls the production
and blending of scents; sweet, bitter, heady, pungent:
the perfume of every kind of flower that has ever
bloomed: the odor of rain on parched ground, of newly dug earth, of newly sawed timber: herbs, baking
bread, pressed grapes, milk and cheese: farm yard
smells, wild animal smells . . . we have them all here,
and a thousand others never dreamed of in your world.
At a perfume symphony, one sits and experiences
subtle gradations of scent, which waft from one side

and another, intermix and react in amazing ways. A whole new world of sensation opened to me when first I was privileged to attend one of these performances.

I cannot omit to mention the area of rhythm. In your world this is usually associated with music, but here rhythm is cultivated in its own right. Viewed interiorly, all life is rhythm, and the flexibility of time here, as compared with time in your world, makes rhythm far more supple. There are rhythmists who perform for us. They use small drums, or clap bits of wood together, and they can keep an audience enthralled by the complex and intricate patterns they produce, merely by these tiny impulses of sound: cross rhythms, off-beat syncopation, and a strange device called *staggering,* by which one player plays, not with the others as they are playing *now,* but with them as they *were* playing in the previous measure! Only those who are expert in this field can follow what is going on, but once you have mastered it you find it most exciting and exhilarating.

Then, of course, there is dancing. Most of us move our bodies rhythmically while singing, to express the sense of the words of the song, but there are some who have developed this faculty to an astonishing degree. As you watch the motion of their bodies and the movement of every limb and muscle, you feel in yourself the joy and wonder and mystery of what they are expressing. The body becomes a flame blown by the Divine Breath, and sets fire to the hearts of all who are in the vicinity. The dancer seems to dissolve into pure love of the Lord, into boundless longing, into utter fulfilment. This is prayer of the highest order, and gets near the inmost shrine of worship.

Excuse me! I see my composer has awakened from his reverie. His meditations (which were conducted in pure music, not words) have inspired him to set forth on the road to heaven. Others are preparing to accompany him, and I must go with them to guide them on the first stage of their journey. Listen to their song: *"We were glad when they said unto us, let us go into the house of the Lord. Our feet shall stand within thy gates, O Jerusalem."* And now they have begun their procession up the green slope, and are invoking the orchestra of heaven to join with them:

"Praise Him with the sound of the trumpet:
Praise Him with the psaltery and harp:
Praise Him with the timbrel and dance:
Praise Him with stringed instruments and organs:
Praise Him upon the loud cymbals,
Praise Him upon the high-sounding cymbals.
Let everything that hath breath praise the Lord,
*   Praise ye the Lord."*

SEVENTEEN

HAPPINESS AND MARRIAGE

HAPPINESS AND MARRIAGE

This is Aqueduct speaking. Greetings, dear friend from the other side! You have found me in a depressed and sour state of mind. To help me overcome my dejection, which is not only affecting myself but also those with whom I associate, the Lord has intimated that I should talk to you about Happiness and Marriage. Very well, I will do so, although it hurts me!

Heavenly Happiness! Some people suppose that just to be in heaven is all that is required to make one happy. "If only we can slip in through St. Peter's gate," they think, "all will be well!" Heaven is indeed a beautiful place. The sweet countryside, the magnificent cities, the gold and silver and precious stones, the river of life . . . But these things alone do not make anyone happy. In fact, it is the other way around: our surroundings are a projection of our own inner states. If we are depressed, the flowers fade and a deep gloom settles over everything. When evil spirits look on heaven, they see nothing but a howling wilderness.

Happiness is a paradox. I well remember a moving picture I once saw. (It was in the boys' house in Nursery-Land.) This picture showed a little boy chasing a butterfly. He threw his cap at it as it settled on the grass, but the cap missed its mark and the butterfly rose and flew further on. Again it settled,

and again the boy threw his cap, but again the butterfly escaped and flew on. And so the boy continued
the futile chase until suddenly there was a sharp cry
from his little sister behind him, who had caught her
dress in a thorn bush. The boy thought, "Oh bother!
I'll just have one more try!" He threw his cap for
the last time, missing the butterfly by inches, and then
abandoned the chase, and turned to help his sister. As
he released her dress and rubbed her scratched knee,
she said softly, "Oh look!" The butterfly had come
back and settled on his shoulder!

Happiness is like that butterfly. To chase it is useless, it will always elude you. But try to help someone else, and it will settle on your shoulder.

Most of us in heaven derive our principal happiness
from our daily work. We all have work to do, which
suits our capabilities, which we enjoy doing, and which
we know is needed in the economy of heaven. Wages?
We receive no wages, nor do we seek any reward, or
even recognition — that is the secret! There is a
maxim we teach our new arrivals in the school here:
*"Heaven begins in a man when he finds delight in
serving others without thought of recompense."* Any
thought of recompense would destroy the happiness
of heaven.

You see we are none of us idle. To have nothing to
do all day would be boring in the extreme; we should
feel we were in hell! The "eternal rest" promised to
us in heaven is not rest from useful activity: it is rest
from anxiety, tension, worry, fear; from temptation
and the itch of self-importance.

Then there is the happiness we derive from communicating our joy to others. This is an ever-expand-
ing field. Already there are some hundreds of people

in my community whom I know intimately, and I try to convey happiness to all of them. And, because I am striving to benefit them, the butterfly settles on my shoulder! I am the one who enjoys it the most! And there is an unexpected by-product to this: they on their side try to give happiness to *me,* and it is quite over-whelming having some hundreds of people all trying to make you happy! You can hardly bear the joy of it! Nor is that the limit. The longer you live in this eternity of the spirit world, the more friends you have — real friends, not merely acquaintances. It becomes thousands, tens of thousands, millions. You have the time here really to get to know people intimately. You get involved in their lives. You lose yourself in them. And they become equally interested in you. And so the circle of love grows wider and wider indefinitely, and with it your happiness increases to eternity.

It says in the Word of God that there is joy among the angels over one sinner that repenteth. How true that is! And there is a great rejoicing when new arrivals enter our community. What banquets we have to welcome them! And how we all compete with one another for the honor and pleasure of helping them to settle in! And if they arrive as husband and wife, then our joy is increased many-fold.

*   *   *   *   *   *

Now it seems I can delay no longer but must face up to the question of marriage in heaven, though it is painful to me personally. As you will realize, all com-plete angels are married pairs. This arrangement has been made by the Lord to prevent any hint of selfish-ness from coming into the atmosphere of heaven: for selfishness is self-destructive.

That is what is holding me back as a single individual. I must be saying "I." Even when I approach the Lord, it is "I" who am approaching Him. When I help others, it is "I" who am doing it. "I, I, I!" Married couples never say "I." They say "We," and that is entirely different from "I." The man does everything he does for the sake of his wife and himself as a team, and she does everything she does for the sake of her husband and herself as a team. They never think of themselves as separate individuals; they cannot do so, for they are interlocked together in a thousand different ways. Do you know that the husband's *thoughts* are actually shared by his wife? Even though she may be temporarily away from him, she still knows exactly what he is thinking. And in the same way, her *affections* are shared by him. Wherever he is, he knows what she is desiring or loving. Together they form an integrated whole. The male is incomplete, the female is incomplete: the unit is a married pair.

Husbands and wives have intercourse together, as on earth, but with far more exquisite pleasure, since spiritual bodies are more sensitive than physical. But no children are born to them. (Your world is the only plane on which children can be born.) Instead of babies, there are births of greater love for the woman and greater intelligence for the man.

People are sometimes puzzled when they discover that angels are married pairs, because of our Lord's remark to the Sadducees: "In the resurrection they neither marry nor are given in marriage, but are as the angels of God in heaven." But remember the context. The Sadducees, who did not believe in a future life, were heckling Jesus with their story of a woman

who was married successively to seven brothers, one
after the other. "Therefore," they asked with sarcasm,
"in the resurrection that you talk about, whose wife
shall she be, for they all had her?" What a picture of
hell! One shrinks with horror from the very thought
of a woman having seven husbands! Is that marriage?
There is surely no such thing in heaven! Here our
marriages are, in a sense, *already made,* for there is
no fundamental character change after death, and it
is possible to ascertain from an examination of a person immediately after his resuscitation where he will
eventually be situated, in heaven or hell. So, from that
point onwards, it is just a question of finding your
consort. Indeed, in the resurrection they neither make
nor break marriages, in the dreadful fashion envisaged
by the Sadducees, but they are *"as the angels of God
in heaven"* — each an indivisible couple.

On earth things are different. Married pairs cannot
be created as such by the Lord, because each partner
must reach his or her heavenly home by the earth-
route, in freedom. To become partners in heaven, they
must have regenerated to the same degree while on
earth. Their inner states must be as nearly as possible
identical, otherwise, according to the laws of attraction
and repulsion operating in the spiritual world, they
could not live together. And regeneration is an individual affair. Thus, the man must be built up as an individual, and the woman must be built up as an individual. A perfect marriage is impossible in your world, because, up to the time of death, each party must be a
free and independent unit, making the individual
choices and decisions necessary for regeneration.

However, if a couple live together on earth as husband and wife, and love each other tenderly, and sincerely want to be united to eternity, then it usually happens that they become consorts together here in the spirit world. They were bent towards each other on earth, and that bending becomes fixed and permanent after death. They are already "one flesh."

Not all cases are so straightforward. There are bound to be problems. Perhaps the process of mutual bending does not take place. Maybe both partners are good at heart, but they are unwilling to lose themselves in one another. Or, one partner may choose the upper way and one the lower, so that they grow further and further apart as they get older, instead of closer and closer together. In that case they will definitely not be partners in the resurrection. How could they be?

Or there is the case where one partner in a happy marriage dies some time before the other, and after he or she has departed the other partner changes interiorly. (There is always the possibility of character change for those living in your world.) When they eventually meet each other over here, they find they can no longer integrate together, because one has changed. Separation is inevitable. He goes to one "place" and she goes to another "place" (place being according to state), and each must thereafter find another consort with whom he or she can be integrated. Always the principle is the same: your partner to eternity will be the member of the opposite sex who, after you have both entered the spiritual world, is nearest to you in your spiritual life.

I did not intend to mention my own personal affairs to you, but perhaps I will do so, by way of illustration. The truth is that my wife on earth has married again.

She has married an old friend of mine. In a way I am glad, because she was very lonely after I left her, and this new companionship will bring happiness to her evening days on earth. But I have to deprive myself of the pleasure of communicating with her, which I have done regularly ever since I came over here, usually during her sleep. In fact, I have decided to cut off all association with her, for I must give her every opportunity to be loyal and loving to her new husband. But this puts me in a very ironical position, for, although I have until now loved her dearly as a wife, my love for her as a person must now drive me to encourage her to become the true wife of another man!

Yet even in this there is a kind of joy — the joy of total self-renunciation and submission to the workings of Providence. I know the Lord loves her and this other man, and me, myself, much more than we love ourselves and one another, and He will overrule everything for the best, taking all the circumstances into account. If she becomes spiritually united with this other man, then in due course the Lord will mercifully allow me to forget her, and will give me some other woman to love and cherish. This I know. "The Lord gives, the Lord takes away, blessed be the name of the Lord."

*   *   *   *   *   *

And so we come to the deepest form of happiness — communing with the Lord. All joy and happiness really come from Him in the first place; these other things are effective only insofar as they open the way for the inflow of His joy. He is infinitely longing to give Himself to us, to unite us with Himself and make us happy from Himself; but He cannot enter us unless we open the way by giving ourselves out to others. The *ego* blocks His entry, as always! But, if we can open ourselves to receive His spirit — then — the deliciousness exceeds anything experienced, even between husband and wife!

Dear Lord, forgive me that I must still say "I." Make it one day "We!"

See, dear friend, my depression has left me! I am happy again! The Sun is brightly shining, and the flowers are lifting their faces. The birds are singing. *Hallelujah! Praise the Lord! Amen.*

Good-bye, and God bless you.

EIGHTEEN

Angelic Choirs

Interview 18

ANGELIC CHOIRS

This is Aqueduct speaking. Greetings, dear friend from the other side! Last night I had the overwhelming experience of seeing the Lord God face to face. This is the second time in my life He has permitted me to do so. But before I attempt to tell you about it, I will say something in a general way concerning our angelic choirs, because it was during a choral celebration that He blessed us with His visible presence.

There is nothing like singing for opening the heart and mind, and most of our people here enjoy singing in small choirs as a form of recreation. Singing is also used for remedial purposes, and choirs are sent to restore order where there is confusion.

We had a choir here recently when we were experiencing some difficulty with a group of new arrivals who were not responding satisfactorily to the usual processes of separation and judgment. They were exceptionally tough, and were being aroused to antagonism by one or two of their number who were demanding to be allowed to go back where they had come from! They sat there sulkily in the Reception Hall, prepared to resist any effort on our part to communicate with them. So I petitioned the Lord to send us some singers to help us establish contact.

A small choir arrived at once, and began to sing.

They were happy and positive and clear-toned, and soon a powerful influence began to be felt. The ring-leaders of opposition turned to listen in spite of themselves. Others, too, began to relax their tensions; the stubborn expression melted from their faces, and a kind of ripple of attentive interest passed through the hall.

The singers were expressing the glorious majesty of the Lord, the Center and Source of all creation, and were suggesting that as we, His children, draw nearer to Him, we also draw nearer to one another; and as we draw near to one another, we draw nearer to Him. The soft all-embracing love that came over through their voices was irresistible. Gradually the company began to divide up into twos and threes. Some shook their fists at the singers and hurried out of the hall — that was to be expected. But the others moved to different sides of the little choir, all facing inwards, and seemed to be drawn in towards it in an ever-closing circle. Then one of the former ringleaders began to sing along with the choir. The sweet flow of harmony continued for a long time, and the effect it produced was like the melting of winter ice under the warm sunshine of spring. Eventually everybody was unashamedly joining in the singing, and moreover their voices were rapidly improving in quality and pitch, and there was quite a remarkable degree of pure harmonization.

After that we had no further trouble with them. They accepted our love, and cooperated happily with us, and in a very short while they had all passed through the preliminary stages of the judgment and were on their way toward heaven. So powerful is the

influence of these angelic choirs that the Lord sometimes sends them to hell itself, to quell insurrection
or rebellion. This seems to be a much better way of
achieving peace and harmony than some of the pro-
cedures adopted by the great powers in your world!

A remarkable feature of our choral singing is that,
so long as the singers are directing their affections
and thoughts towards the Lord, their voices harmonize
together perfectly, even though each individual vocal-
ist is, as it were, improvizing on the selected theme.
Because of this, choirs from different regions of heaven can meet together and sing concordantly, without
rehearsal. Their voices are quite different in tone quality, yet they blend beautifully together. And the more
choirs there are, and the greater variety in their tone
quality, the more beautiful and complex will be the
resulting harmony.

No individual singer in these angelic choirs ever
wishes to surpass the others or take a lead. If anyone
did this, he would dissociate himself at once. Rather,
they all sing together as a team. Nor do they require a
conductor, since every member of the choir is looking
intently to the Lord Himself. God is the only Maestro
in heaven!

If any singer turns his thoughts away from the
Lord and thinks admiringly of his own voice and musical abilities, discord immediately arises and the
whole ensemble collapses. But this rarely happens
with those who have had any singing experience, because we soon discover how little we ourselves con-
tribute to the beauty of what we are producing, and
how we are only instruments, as it were, played by the
hand and breath of the Lord Himself.

Both male and female singers constitute these choirs. Naturally, the women sing with a sweeter tone than the men, because their affections are more delicate and sensitive. The men's affections are direct and powerful, so that when men and women sing together, the men furnish the melody, and the women harmonize it, just as wives harmonize the lives of their husbands. The melody is in the bass. Unmarried girls, however, who have not yet found their future partners, are not yet in the harmony stage, and we hear them singing the sweetest songs together in pure melodic line.

O course, we do not have to be members of a choir to sing! We all sing a great deal, all the time, at our work, during our recreation, while travelling ... whenever we think of a truth and it stirs us emotionally. How could we hold ourselves back?

But the great choirs are what move me most. And now I must tell you about what happened last night. There was a big united worship service in our city, to which I and some others from our village were invited. About three thousand were present, in a large auditorium. The Holy Spirit was working powerfully among us; we were in an exalted state of communion with the Lord and with one another. After a reading from the Word, one of the ministers who was leading our devotions said, quite unexpectedly: "Let us praise the Lord, each in his own way; let there be a General Glorification." At once people began to say, from a full heart: *"Praise the Lord! Glorify His Name! O Lord, how great are Thy works! The Lord reigneth, let the earth rejoice!"* and so on. They were speaking very softly at first, like a gentle murmur. Soon a musical note seemed to form itself from their voices, then another forming a chord, then another, until a warm glow of harmony began to fill the auditorium, floating up into the air and pressing against the roof.

And then the tremendous thing happened. The roof dissolved away, and we were standing in the open air, with the clear vault of the sky spread above us. A dazzling rose-colored light seemed to swing over to the east, and far away we could hear a kind of echo to our singing. The angels in that whole region were joining with us. It was a sonorous tone, at first like the cooing of doves, but increasing in power till it resembled the blast of trumpets filling the whole sky.

Then the light swung round to the south, becoming violet in color; and the angels in that region were caught up in the general glorification, taking fire from our flame. Their song began like the flutter of birds' wings, but grew and increased until it resembled the tremendous sweep of violins.

The other quarters of the sky, west and north, were now lit up with a bright green light, and the singing came from them, sounding like reed instruments and flutes. So the angelic orchestra was complete.

And, in the center of the firmanent, far overhead, the light began to swirl around in great circles, with the colors of a rainbow, until in the center of it all, I saw ... our beloved Lord Himself, looking down at each one of us so benignly, raising His hand to bless us. And, as when I saw my Lord before, by the bank of the river, the air was filled with a strong fragrance of flowers.

NINETEEN

COMMUNING WITH GOD

Interview 19

COMMUNING WITH GOD

This is Aqueduct speaking. Greetings, dear friend from the other side! I believe I said something to you at our last meeting about having been privileged to look into the face of our beloved Lord. Since that awesome experience, strange things have been happening to me, which have led me to perceive that I am shortly to undergo a change of state. I shall then be no longer able to communicate with you, nor you with me. Our little experiment will therefore have to come to an end. I shall regret its termination, as I have keenly enjoyed our relationship together, though it has been rather bizarre. (I can still see right through your body if I look at you intently!) I am informed that you are to visit me once more, after which we shall not meet again until you leave your earthly body and come over here through the normal process of "death."

Though you will be unable to communicate with me, I hope and believe you will continue to draw closer and closer to the Lord our heavenly Father, and that you will use your influence on earth to encourage others to do the same, for He is the Source of life, happiness, and peace. The most direct way to do this is by prayer.

Prayer is basic to any kind of religion, and yet it seems to be largely misunderstood by most people who come over from your world, even religious people. And, looking back, I am sure I misunderstood it myself. We thought that prayer was begging some favor from God, asking Him to give us something we wanted. We supposed that out prayers would change God's actions in some way. I guess we thought of Him as being like a worldly monarch, who might be persuaded to pay attention to us if only we worried Him enough or bribed Him with flattery. But, my dear friend, anyone with any insight must realize that the Lord, the Creator of the universe, does not need to have His attention drawn to our needs, nor can He be cajoled and persuaded to do things for us which He would not do if we left Him alone!

God is omniscient. He knows every one of us, oh so much better than we know ourselves! And He loves us, oh so much more deeply and truly than we love ourselves! Moreover, He can see into eternity and plan for our eternal welfare, of which we are ignorant. Will He only help us if we pray to Him to do so? That is preposterous! Even a human parent loves his children and finds his greatest joy in their welfare; how much more will our heavenly Father seek our good!

Prayer is not intended to alter God, but rather to establish proper relations with God. It helps us to receive the blessings He has prepared for us. The table is laid, the banquet is spread; but we have to stretch out our hands and take what we need.

Actually, only a small part of prayer is asking for specific things. This is not its main purpose. Its main purpose is to open up our end of the channel or pipeline which connects Him with us, so that His life may flow freely into us and through us. True prayer is a two-way communion between a man and his heavenly Father. It is *talking with God*.

We are told we must "pray without ceasing," and even in a busy life this is easier to do than is generally supposed. Whenever there is a gap in the time-sequence of your lives, you should turn your thoughts inward and talk with God: between two appointments, while travelling from place to place; resting after a meal; lying in bed. He will guide you when you are in difficulty, doubt or confusion, by setting your thoughts in order. He will comfort you when you are lonely or dejected; strengthen you when you are tempted or feel inadequate; give you peace when you are disturbed, and joy when you are sad. Constant prayer will accustom you to His presence and open the whole spiritual area of your mind, so that when eventually you enter the spiritual world you will feel at home and at ease. Prayer will help you also in your relations with other people. As you pray for others, the Lord's life and healing will flow through you as a channel, and enter them, as it were, by the side door. And it will help you to love your enemies, for how can you hate those for whom you are praying? "Love your enemies, bless them that curse you, do good to them that hate you, and pray for them which despitefully use you and persecute you, that ye may be the children of your Father which is in heaven"; and very soon you will find you are regarding them as brothers!

Some people find it embarrassing to pray because they think God is too far off to be able to hear them. He is not far off. He is within you! It is an amazing fact, that the Lord who created the heavens and the earth, actually dwells personally and fully in that little vessel within us which we call the soul. If He withdrew for one instant, we should cease to be ourselves. It is because He dwells within us that we are in His image and likeness, human beings and not animals. It is for this same reason that we live to eternity. And if you ask me *how* God can be fully present within every one of His billions of children, in your world and ours, while at the same time He is controlling the universe, I can only reply that He is infinite, and therefore outside the limitations of space; and that the Divine is not a quantity but a quality. The infinite is indivisible. Wherever God is present at all, He is present in fulness.

Since the Lord is thus fully present within each of us, why are so few people in your world aware of Him? Because you all begin your adult lives with only the natural degree of your minds open — the area of thought and will concerned with self and the world. The main purpose of life is to rise up from this natural degree, and pass successively through higher and higher planes of being, until at last you reach so close to the partition that separates you from God that you are caught up in His vibrating sphere; you can hear His voice, and feel the loving pressure of His hand. In your world it is indeed difficult to achieve this nearness to God; but when you come over here at death you will find you can be purified and simplified to such a degree that you will be left with nothing except that partition!

It is the borderline or frontier between the infinite and the finite, across which nothing normally passes. No ordinary human being can merge with the Divine. Jesus Christ did it because His Soul WAS GOD, whereas your soul is only a vessel containing God.

The idea that we might become Divine is appalling, horrifying. Even the highest angels are perpetually and joyfully conscious of the fact that they are only vessels containing God, that their life comes from Him and is His life in them. Their outstanding quality consists in that they have been stripped bare of every other feeling! They have no will of their own, apart from the Lord's will, and no thoughts apart from His thoughts. They are His, and He is theirs. They are a finite replica of His infinity, linked up with Him at every point of contact. Oh how I yearn to become like that!

* * * * * *

Soon I must take my leave of you, dear friend. This encourages me to open up a little, and share with you my most recent experience, which I interpret as a preparation for my forthcoming change of state. What happened was this: the Lord allowed me to penetrate for a few moments through that partition of which I have been speaking, the frontier between the finite and the infinite. Whether it was a dream or a vision, or what it was, I cannot tell. It came to me without my seeking it.

I was lying quietly on my bed at home, meditating on the love of God, and praying with deep concentration that I might draw nearer to Him. Suddenly, I felt myself being lifted up high into the sky. Above me was a layer of cloud covering the entire firmament like a solid ceiling. I knew that this cloud was the limit of human consciousness. Above it was the Divine, below it was man. The cloud moderated the downflow of energy from God, and enabled man to have evil thoughts and feelings without being endangered by

God's holiness — as happens, of course, in hell. Now, as I gazed up, I noticed a kind of welcoming brightness; there was glory in the cloud. I realized I was to see God as He really is. In the past, when I have seen Him, He has come down to me, adapting Himself to my state; now I was to go up to Him.

How can I describe in words what is actually beyond thought? The only way is to continue with the cloud symbolism. As I was lifted higher and higher, I eventually entered the cloud. A kind of vaporous darkness closed around me. I trembled with a nameless fear, and my hair rose on my head. Then I emerged on the other side, and was for a moment blinded. Light surrounded me, solid light. It seemed to press on me; a deluge of light atoms, falling down like a heavy rain. As I grew accustomed to the brightness, I found I was in a world of flame and color. Music, at first sweet, grew louder and louder until it almost deafened me. Beneath, on my lower side, all was blackness and nothingness, but on my upper side the rays of the sun beat so painfully that I thought I was being destroyed. But it was a delicious agony. Then a voice boomed out, and I found I was having a dialogue with God, but not as it had ever been before. In the past, all my prayers had been spoken in my language, the language of finite thought; but now I was speaking in His language. For one sparkling moment I partook of His infinity and eternity. I saw the universe through His mind; I shared His omniscience, omnipotence and all-embracing love. The ecstasy was too great; I swooned. In a state of semi-consciousness I felt myself being let down, very gently, till I was back on my bed at home. I was safe again in my finitude, back in the created universe, content forever to be a vessel of life, not life itself. Outside the house, a gentle haze covered the landscape, and the sun shone serenely, far away before my eyes, turning the atmosphere to gold.

* * * * * *

I shall never be the same again. I have been cauterized. My inessentials have been burnt away. Little remains now, except my relationship with God.

Something is holding me back. Somebody is holding me back. I need a partner, a consort. When I have found my consort, whoever she is, it will be "God and us," a love relationship of perfect completeness and fulfilment. We shall be able to go forward together.

How amazing to think that everybody has this glorious region of infinity within himself, this radiancy above all conscious thought. Tell your friends on earth about it. Always remember that the Lord, Himself, is very near: overwhelmingly powerful and beautiful, but immediately accessible to those who love Him.

Lord, I adore You, I worship You! Use my body as You will, for it is Yours. Enfill and use my mind! Pour the water of Your truth over me and into me! If only I, as an Aqueduct, can convey something of this water to those who are athirst, on earth or over here, or in some other region of the spirit, as You will, then I shall be content . . . .

TWENTY

RECEDING VISION

Interview 20

RECEDING VISION

This is Aqueduct Speaking. Are you there, friend from the other side? Can you hear me? I cannot see you. Yes, now I can see you.

I have come to say good-bye. God bless you. I hope you will one day be as happy as I am now. Happy!

* * * * * *

The Lord has moved me on. I am in another state of life. Another work. Everything progresses. Everything is wonderful . . . .

* * * * * *

Listen. Can you hear me? My consort was awaiting me in this new place! The most beautiful woman — young, fragrant. The Lord has united us. We are one. Henceforth it is "WE," not "I." Praise the Lord!

* * * * * *

Who? Why, none other! My own wife from the old world! More beautiful than in our courting days!

* * * * * *

How my heart sings! Hallelujah! Salvation, glory, honor, power, be unto our God!

Blessing, glory, wisdom, thanksgiving . . . .

Forever and ever . . . .